★The★

HOME FRONT

DEVOTIONAL

"With a deeply intuitive understanding of the joys and struggles of military life, Tara McMullen uplifts military-affiliated families to understand more profoundly that our identity does not derive from a military career, offering of exhaustive volunteer hours, or wearing shiny unit pins or patches, but from God's unabashed love for us as his sons and daughters. McMullen has created a prayerful, witty, beautifully written, and spiritually meaningful resource to help us grow in relationship with Jesus, in family life, and in faith-filled friendships that bind military communities. I highly recommend this book for insight and reflection."

Elizabeth Tomlin
General Counsel for the Archdiocese for the Military Services, USA

"The gift Tara McMullen offers military spouses with this book is truly a beautiful one! This lifestyle often feels lonely, turbulent, and scary, and she uses scripture to wrap us up in comfort, clarity, and unwavering love. This book is exactly what we have been craving in the military community—we wish we would have had it when starting our journeys as military spouses years ago!"

Jen Ferrell and Kirst Navaroli
Cofounders of Wives of the Armed Forces

"Tara McMullen offers a welcome tool to navigate the rigors of military family life. She recognizes the essential role of faith in responding to a demanding path both for the member of the Armed Forces and the family."

Most Rev. Timothy P. Broglio
Archbishop for the Military Services, USA

"Brimming with humor and authenticity, Tara McMullen's insights and stories are laser-tailored to the unique, demanding, and rewarding life of a Catholic military spouse. This book is an invaluable companion for individuals and Catholic chapel groups who are seeking to draw strength from the richness of their Catholic faith, especially when their loved ones are called away."

Fr. Mike Palmer, CSC
US Army Chaplain

⋆The⋆ HOME FRONT DEVOTIONAL

Navigate Military Life with Courage, Hope, and Faith

TARA MCMULLEN

Nihil Obstat: Reverend Monsignor Michael Heintz, PhD
Censor Librorum
Imprimatur: Most Reverend Kevin C. Rhoades
Bishop of Fort Wayne–South Bend
Given at Fort Wayne, Indiana, on September 24, 2024

The *Nihil Obstat* and *Imprimatur* are official declarations that a book or pamphlet is free of doctrinal or moral error. No implication is contained therein that those who have granted the *Nihil Obstat* or *Imprimatur* agree with its contents, opinions, or statements expressed.

Founded in 1865, Ave Maria Press is a ministry of the United States Province of Holy Cross.

www.avemariapress.com

Paperback: ISBN-13 978-1-64680-354-5

E-book: ISBN-13 978-1-64680-355-2

Cover image © Devin Justesen/Unsplash.

Cover and text design by Andy Wagoner.

Printed and bound in the United States of America.

Library of Congress Cataloging-in-Publication Data is available.

FOR TRENT,

who dragged me into this.

AND FOR OUR CHILDREN,

whom we dragged along with us.

CONTENTS

Introduction: You Are a Lifeboat ix

1. Identity + Belovedness 1

2. Marriage + Change 11

3. Friendship + Sainthood 19

4. TDY + Consistency 29

5. Parenting + Knowing Jesus 39

6. Assignments + Trust 49

7. Moving + Presence 57

8. The Hard Parts + Shelter 63

9. Pre-Deployment Prep + Patience 69

10. Deployment + Hope 77

11. Service + Servant Heart 85

12. The Future + Re-Discernment 93

Conclusion: You Are a Willow 103

Bibliography 107

Ξ Introduction

YOU ARE A LIFEBOAT

My Air Force husband will hate that I am starting this book with a naval analogy, but here we go: If you've ever ridden on a cruise ship or any other large ship, you've seen the rows and rows of lifeboats. You've been trotted out to the deck to go over the safety procedures, how to put on your life vest, how to enter the craft in an orderly fashion without things devolving into pandemonium, etc. Then you probably didn't consider the lifeboats for the rest of your trip. Knowing they were there was enough.

For many of my early years as a military wife, I felt like the lifeboat. While I knew deep down I played a critical, if not life-saving, role in our family's journey, I often felt as if I was just along for the ride. While my husband, the cruise ship, charted our course, negotiated our destinations, and motored us from here to there, I bounced along with the stream, occasionally glancing at the wake below, knowing it wasn't truly mine.

The cruise ship doesn't have it easy either. He has to stay afloat at all times so the lifeboat isn't needed. If he makes an error, the crew has to follow his path. He feels the weight of all those passengers, plus their individual baggage, every day. In some ways, it's easier to be the life raft. It only occasionally involves real stress or duty.

But then I started to get an inkling that maybe I was called to more than riding a wave.

Traditionally, the role of a military wife was to hold down the home front. To sew patches on flight suits, to host social events, to watch the neighbor's kids, to volunteer at the pharmacy, to bake, to pray, to comfort. While there are valuable elements of that role that appealed to me—namely, bringing new parents a hot meal, sending condolence cards, hosting a community-building beer trolley—others felt outdated and grated at my small dose of feminism, my dreams, and frankly, my self-worth. Try as I might to fit that mold, it didn't feel authentic me.

As I teased out the differences between playing a role and fulfilling a calling, I had to take a hard look at my own suppositions.

To what am I called as a Christian? Whom do I owe? How do I act?

What do I think the calling of a wife and mother looks like? What does Jesus say that looks like?

What about as a friend? A fellow military spouse? How do I love and serve the people around me?

How do I endure the unique challenges of military life with an unabashedly Christian perspective?

And finally, what about my gifts as a writer? How do I use those gifts to serve?

This book, I hope, is one of those ways.

For me, the process of discerning where God is, where faith is, and where the military family's life purpose is was a hard one. The process was, and remains, years long. It changes with seasons and scenarios, with friendships and failures. It has at times been filled with community and at others been very lonely. I imagine your journey isn't so different.

There was a period, during our long tenure in North Carolina, when a group of Catholic military spouses and I met for what started as a weekly Bible study, but morphed into more of a monthly Catholic book club as time and commitments and schedules got in the way. Still, we'd choose a book that had tenets that appealed to us—motherhood, sainthood, faith, the Holy Spirit, friendship—and dive into a discussion that allowed us to reflect together on that theme. That little community inspired this book.

That period was perhaps the first time I shared my faith, my questions, my hopes with a group of like-minded women. It stirred in me a desire for all my friendships to have the depth, the vulnerability, and the honesty that was inspired in those gatherings.

Now, we didn't always agree. We didn't even always get along. But in nurturing these relationships through Christ, through faith and through love, they just seemed to be molded in a different clay than other friendships. We have all since been flung to different corners of the globe, and many of those friendships have withered because of distance and personalities, but still, when someone needs a prayer or a boost, that group text comes alive. It is a sisterhood both rooted and matured in faith. My humble hope is that this book, when used for genuine self-reflection and then vulnerable and honest sharing, can re-create that community. Your shared experiences in military families can bring you together, but your shared faith can bind you.

Despite several years studying together, we never did find a book that seamlessly intersected our Catholic faith with our roles in military families. Books often contained one or the other, but that place where the two came together seemed elusive. Maybe this book can be a launching point for that conversation.

As you walk through these pages, know I am no biblical expert. I have no degree in divinity or theology or Latin. I am just a wife, a mother, a sister, a daughter, a friend, and a

Catholic who tries, and often fails, to set Jesus as her guiding star, every day.

You should also know I'm not a plucky optimist. I won't tell you to silver-line all your challenges, for there are many in this lifestyle. But when they become hard to bear, I will tell you, probably repeatedly, that God didn't offer us an easy life. He didn't even offer *his own son* an easy life. Instead, Jesus hung on a cross so we could experience his loving embrace, his forgiveness, and his acceptance.

Given that this book is about emulating Jesus in our own meek and humble ways, it has twelve chapters for a few reasons:

First, Jesus chose twelve disciples, so twelve chapters seemed a fitting launching point. There are also twelve months. If you're using this book for both self-reflection and group conversation, which I'd highly recommend for reasons we'll get to shortly, it seems you could meet once each month to discuss one chapter's theme. This would be a leisurely pace and allow for significant self-reflection and prayer. And it would make space for regular military life, with its pop-up surprises, to occur in between chapters.

Alternatively, you could read a chapter per week, and finish in a quarter. That also seems nice and round and tidy, which is how I aspire to live my life.

Yet again, you could read a chapter a day, and take a break for the Sabbath, and you'd finish in two weeks. I wouldn't, as I lack the discipline and routine to do something every single day, but maybe this tempo works for you.

These twelve chapters are organized by milestones in the life of a military family, from those early days of marriage to the retirement finish line. You don't have to have experienced them yet—there's still value in considering how faraway milestones might dictate your decision-making now.

You may have experienced some of these milestones years ago, or even decades ago. Reflecting on how they've changed you, your family, and your course can be rich, even years later. Or you may be in the thick of many of these milestones all at once. I've been there. I *am* there. Bask in those chapters, but I'd also suggest that you return to them in a few months, in a few years, and see how things have changed. The beauty of answering the reflection questions on paper means you can watch your own transformation over time.

Or, you may not be in a military family. You may have a child who is in the military. Perhaps you have a friend who is a military spouse. Or maybe you are a compassionate individual who wants to learn more about this lifestyle, or just someone who sees their own story reflected in some, if not all, of these chapters. You're all welcome and I'm happy you found this book.

Each chapter, in addition to being centered on a military milestone, is rooted in a Catholic or Christian text. We'll start each chapter with an excerpt that encapsulates an important theme or idea, and then throughout the chapter we'll return to that excerpt or others in the text. These are rich resources, but I've kept them short here because I know there are phases of life where sitting with even just a line or two of religious text can feel like a herculean effort. And yet, in other seasons, you may crave the intellectual or spiritual stimulation of a challenge. If that's the case, I'd recommend you go read the reference text in full. Some are heavy and daunting at first, but broken down and ingested piece by piece, line by line, can be beautifully rich.

That's also the beauty of doing this in a group. Some people will stretch themselves and can offer context from further explorations. Others will bask in just a line or two and have deep revelations to share. Some will come with many questions and notes. Others will bring the muffins and nurture the social aspect of the group. These are all valuable roles! Having a group that spans a wide range of experiences will offer diversity of thought, intent, and curiosity. Those distinct outlooks will hopefully push you to see beyond your own and widen your aperture even more.

You may also notice my references are Air Force-centric, if not specifically pilot-centric. That's the language in which I am semi-fluent, but I've done my best (with some help) to translate this for folks in the Army, Navy, Marines, Coast Guard, Space Force, or even elsewhere in the Air Force. Despite the wide range of experiences that fall under the unwieldy "military life" umbrella, we are still enduring something unique together. I hope the experiences and stories I share can be a lens through which you see your own, no matter where your service to our nation has taken you.

As you move through these pages, know I am living and learning alongside you. And I'm praying with you and for you. This life is so very challenging, but also so rich.

Ξ Chapter 1

IDENTITY + BELOVEDNESS

> As the Father has loved me, so have I loved you; abide in my love. If you keep my commandments, you will abide in my love, just as I have kept my Father's commandments and abide in his love. These things I have spoken to you, that my joy may be in you, and that your joy may be full. This is my commandment, that you love one another as I have loved you.
>
> —John 15:9–12

From the moment you tickle the edge of military life, you realize titles are important. Private. Sergeant. Ensign. Lieutenant. Major. Colonel. General.

Then come the fields or positions.

And a base or squadron or platoon.

It often feels like I'm taxonomically classifying my husband as part of a National Geographic special where I name his family, genus, and species in a whispery British accent: "Ah, an elusive F-15 pilot from the fighter pilot family, hailing from the 336th squadron of the sandy fields of Seymour Johnson. They are a rare breed. Notice the confident gait, called 'swagger' . . ."

Jokes aside, his identity is crafted and patched all over him. But for military families, that identity gets muddy.

Military spouses face an unemployment rate over 20 percent, nearly seven times the national average. The loss of income can be devastating, but so too can the loss of the thing you worked for, studied for, strived for. It may feel like you're squandering your gifts, or losing what was unequivocally *yours*. Or maybe you haven't yet had an opportunity to define yourself, and rolled into this life just as you were coming of age. Or maybe you've had to chameleon yourself to the bases and places and opportunities that have been presented, and in all that change, you've lost sight of who you truly are.

In any case, there's a temptation to identify with your active-duty spouse's job—and many military families do—but pinning your identity on theirs feels fraught, even if "dependent" is listed next to your name on every piece of identification and official form. Defining yourself by someone else's actions can be a precarious, if not inauthentic, foundation on which to build your life. It can also reinforce the unnecessary divisions—such as enlisted or officer, Air Force or Army—that fly in the face of our Christian call to community.

Other military spouses identify purely with parenthood, if not by choice, by situation. Being a stay-at-home parent isn't required in this life, but it feels that way when your active-duty spouse's schedule is erratic, or when they disappear for weeks or months at a time. The other parent is almost always the one to caretake on sick days, to stay home during school breaks, or to fill the summer hours. But staking an identity in a role defined by small (and not always grateful) people can feel one-sided.

So who are we?

For so many years after marrying my husband, I wrestled with this question.

I had been a classic overachiever—a perfectionist and hustler who helped put herself through Notre Dame. I had aspirations of working at a magazine—which I did—until marriage into the military derailed a traditional professional ascent. Rural North Carolina didn't afford a lot of opportunities for magazine-writing, or writing of any sort, or even working. At least not at first. And so I resented that marriage, though blissful, took away something I had worked hard for, and identified with for much of my life. Even though I was endlessly proud of him and his career path, it was grating that it had, in so many ways, usurped and outpaced my own.

I threw myself into volunteering: I worked the base auction, cooked and delivered countless meals to families with new babies or surgeries or losses, co-created a Bible study-turned-book club, hosted social events. I became a key spouse for our squadron, a role that serves as a volunteer liaison between military leadership and families. I had a baby. And another.

And still, I no longer felt like me. I no longer knew myself.

My experience is not unique; it's not even unique to military life. Scroll through any mommy blog and you'll see mentions of a loss of identity. Talk to any veteran and you'll hear the questions in their voice when they talk about leaving the service. Talk to a civilian who has been laid off and you'll see the pain in their eyes from being told they aren't doing or being what or whom they thought they were.

And that's the problem with staking our lives in earthly titles. They are temporary, imaginary, typically externally defined, and so very finite. They are also often wedged deep in our pride, our self-worth, our relationships. Digging them out is hard and painful. But when we can prune those weeds, what remains is a singular truth: We are beloved. And we are invited to "remain in [that] love" (John 15:9).

That may seem a simple concept, but what if we could truly, deeply root ourselves in that call? What if we believed, deep in our beings, that we are sons and daughters of a Father who loves us, cherishes us, seeks us, calls us? That we don't need to earn that love? What if we trusted that perfect love is all we need? What if we lived steeped in that love every day, in every action, in every breath? What would our lives look like? What would we look like? I imagine it would look like the true Christian vocation.

It's hard to envision what that kind of love looks like. Imagine your most intimate relationship with your spouse or parent or child or best friend. That love is nurturing, fulfilling, comforting, yes? But does it also have flaws? Are there moments, even small ones, in that relationship where you feel misunderstood, small, or unloved? Most likely. And so it's hard to trust that our relationship with God is pure, unearned, unabashed love.

Not long ago, I had an experience in one of my deepest relationships that brought up those feelings of inadequacy, invisibility, unlovability. I took those feelings to God. As I sat in a sunlit Catholic church in silent adoration, I prayed about how I was feeling, why I felt that way, why it hurt to feel that way. And without thinking I prayed, "God, if I don't feel loved by the people you have given me on Earth, how will I ever feel worthy of your love?" And without a pause this thought reverberated: "You aren't asked to be worthy of my love. I called you anyway." As I stared at the cross, I finally internalized what a profound love we are invited into.

God sent his son to die for us not because we were deserving, or good, or working hard, or on the right path. He sent him regardless of those things. We were sent a savior out of true, unconditional love. We were sent someone who claimed us while fully knowing our deepest sins, flaws, and failings.

I thought of my relationship with my own children. As their mother, I'd contend I know them better than any other earthly being. I know their temperaments. I know their flaws. I know when they are prone to disobedience or tantrums or unkind words. Do I love them in spite of those shortcomings? Absolutely. Now, do I do the same for my neighbors? Do I love the people in my life who make me feel small or weak or angry? Can I say my response is just as generous? I honestly cannot.

I cannot look to Jesus on the Cross, arms outstretched, heart unguarded, and say I show the same kind of vulnerable love with everyone in my life.

But emulating that generous love is what we are called to do. If we believe we are loved by God such that we are part of the Body of Christ, part of his Church, then we are both invited and responsible for bringing others into that Body through raising and teaching our own families, loving our neighbors, being witnesses to the Christian life, evangelizing, being charitable and generous, being salt, being light, being an extension of Christ in all that we do, in all that we are. In short, we are asked to carry on the work of love that Jesus began, and that he sent his apostles to continue.

That is both a remarkably simple and hugely overwhelming call.

But we see it again and again in the Bible. What does Jesus ask of us? He tells Peter, our role model, to "feed my sheep"

(John 21:15–17). He tells his followers to tend the vineyard (Matthew 21:33). He even sums it up for us in that passage from the Gospel of John when he tells us that we are to "love one another as I have loved you."

We are not called to titles. We are not called to successes. We are not called to promotions or bonuses (though they are nice!). We are called to love and be loved, and to let the rest of our lives flow through that love.

Should that seem ambiguous and unwieldy, Jesus is even more specific. In the passage from the Gospel of John that opened this chapter, we hear his call to love and serve others—in this passage from the Gospel of Matthew, he reveals to us how we are to do that:

> When the Son of Man comes in his glory, and all the angels with him, then he will sit on the throne of his glory. All the nations will be gathered before him, and he will separate people one from another as a shepherd separates the sheep from the goats, and he will put the sheep at his right hand and the goats at the left. Then the king will say to those at his right hand, "Come, you that are blessed by my Father, inherit the kingdom prepared for you from the foundation of the world; for I was hungry and you gave me food, I was thirsty and you gave me something to drink, I was a stranger and you welcomed me, I was naked and you gave me clothing, I was sick and you took care of me, I was in prison and you visited me." Then the righteous will answer him, "Lord, when was it that we saw you hungry and gave you food, or thirsty and gave you something to drink? And when was it that we

> saw you a stranger and welcomed you, or naked and gave you clothing? And when was it that we saw you sick or in prison and visited you?" And the king will answer them, "Truly I tell you, just as you did it to one of the least of these who are members of my family, you did it to me." (Matthew 25:40)

Who are the people in our lives who are hungry? Who are thirsty? Who are sick or imprisoned or alone? Who needs the light of Christ brought to them—not in a pushy evangelical way, but in pure love and presence?

Our actions need not be extravagant. We can regularly contribute to the parish food drive. We can donate our secondhand baby clothes to new parents. We can call the lonely relative even though they irk us. We can make space at our table for the friend who has hurt us. We just need to continually seek out those in need.

Maybe it's you who is in need right now. Maybe in the bustle of this life, you can no longer hear God's voice, can no longer feel his embrace. Maybe you feel too weak to be his hands. Too dark to bear his light. That's okay.

In the time after I had my first baby, and quickly after, my second, I felt this kind of helplessness. I had long been a do-er. I was capable, productive, helpful. These were attributes that I prided myself on. When I suddenly became sleep-deprived and homebound with a newborn, a pandemic, and then another newborn, I no longer felt I had the capacity to help others. In fact, I suddenly needed the help of others. And being the receiver didn't feel nearly as good as the giver.

A friend who writes beautiful weekly emails about the heart of faith sent a reflection one day about how our relationships ought to be like a symphony. She wrote about complementary differences and melodies, how a flute and a tuba can play dramatically different roles, but both serve the harmony of the whole. It got me thinking: What if I was in a season of musical rest? What if other instruments were playing around me while I held still for a time? And what if in allowing others to shine, the symphony was better in the end?

And it was. It was hard to be vulnerable. It was hard to say yes to help, to meals, to hand-me-downs for my babies who seemed to grow out of clothing every few weeks, to playdates I didn't want to go to because I was tired. But those relationships became richer when I started being authentic and humble and genuinely thankful. When I started delighting in the wisdom of others instead of becoming jealous or feeling less-than. When I allowed myself to abide in their generous love.

And then, when time and energy and sleep returned, I went back to serving others—not because I believed I needed to earn their love, God's love, or my own self-love, but because I knew from experience what genuine love and help looked like.

Now, my version of service may not be yours. Perhaps you're a saxophone or a clarinet or a timpani in our symphonic metaphor. If we draw close to God, he will show us when and how he wants us to serve.

We must take the time in prayer to know ourselves, to know whom God has designed us to be, the talents he has bestowed upon us, and the ways he hopes to use us. Once we grow in tune with that voice, once we turn our hearts to God, then we can pour out our love in the way God intended.

Questions for Reflection

1. Think of the patches you wear to define or label yourself to others. Does that identity take into consideration your true vocation?
2. How does God's love shape your life? How do you feel that love? How could you become more aware of it?
3. How are you actively choosing to love God?
4. How are you loving and serving those around you in accordance with your gifts?
5. What are new and tangible things you could add to your service?
6. For further exploration on the role of lay people as defined by the Church, consider the Vatican II document *Lumen Gentium*. In chapter 4, "The Laity," we read:

> But the laity, by their very vocation, seek the kingdom of God by engaging in temporal affairs and by ordering them according to the plan of God. They live in the world, that is, in each and in all of the secular professions and occupations. They live in the ordinary circumstances of family and social life, from which the very web of their existence is woven. They are called there by God that by exercising their proper function and led by the spirit of the Gospel they may work for the sanctification of the world from within as a leaven. In this way they may make Christ known to others, especially by the testimony of a life resplendent in faith, hope and charity. Therefore, since they are tightly bound up in all types of

> temporal affairs it is their special task to order and to throw light upon these affairs in such a way that they may come into being and then continually increase according to Christ to the praise of the Creator and the Redeemer.

How might you be called to be leaven in the place where God has placed you in this moment of your life? How might you "work for the sanctification of the world from within"?

Ξ Chapter 2

MARRIAGE + CHANGE

> If I speak in the tongues of men or of angels, but do not have love, I am only a resounding gong or a clanging cymbal. If I have the gift of prophecy and can fathom all mysteries and all knowledge, and if I have a faith that can move mountains, but do not have love, I am nothing. If I give all I possess to the poor and give over my body to hardship that I may boast, but do not have love, I gain nothing. Love is patient, love is kind. It does not envy, it does not boast, it is not proud. It does not dishonor others, it is not self-seeking, it is not easily angered, it keeps no record of wrongs. Love does not delight in evil but rejoices with the truth. It always protects, always trusts, always hopes, always perseveres. Love never fails.
>
> —1 Corinthians 13:1–8

I remember our Pre-Cana marriage preparation experience so clearly. Since we were to be married in my home parish in the Chicago suburbs, my diocese prescribed a one-day marriage preparation extravaganza alongside thirty or so other couples. So on a slushy winter Saturday, Trent and I both traveled to Chicago to sit in a drafty parish basement as we put on paper how we thought our marriage might go.

Because we are both type A personalities, and because I spend my professional life interviewing people, we had already discussed most of the prescribed topics (faith, family planning, communication, etc.) top to bottom, inside and out, along with a list of what-ifs and worst-case scenarios. We were prepared.

As I recall, the last topic before the lunch break was finances. We, perhaps blessedly, had none. In fact, we had negative funds if we took into consideration my school and car loans, so it made no difference to us if we combined our barren bank accounts or not. But the couple next to us was at least a decade our senior, so finances were a sticking point. A loud one. And we were meant to discuss this topic with others at our table. Yikes. I remember scurrying away from their argument wondering how they hadn't considered the topic before this public moment.

It's a moment of arrogance I've come back to many times in our almost decade of marriage. Scenarios arise and often I respond so very differently from what I scribbled down on that form many years ago. And that's the best gift my husband has given me in nearly a decade of marriage: the opportunity for change. In a cancel culture where you're struck down for any misstep or mistake or for reversing your position—even when the amendment is because you've learned better—change is a rare and precious commodity.

Once upon that Pre-Cana form, I'm sure I wrote that we planned to have many children, and I would stay home and raise them while he served twenty years in the military. Four years later, about six weeks into motherhood, I realized that this vision wasn't quite right. I immediately craved the mental and creative stimulation writing offered. It became clear to me that I could not channel all my frenetic energy into feeding and sleep schedules, eczema treatments, or silly songs. It took many more weeks before I tearfully confessed to my husband that I didn't want to quit work. In fact, I possibly wanted to work *more.*

It took even longer to explain to him that writing was helping me both understand and articulate who I was becoming, who *we* were becoming. Writing let me capture and savor little moments, even the ones that were hard or painful, and later string them together to better see the bigger picture coming into view. Even mundane projects allowed me a few moments for myself, to let my brain exercise in ways I hadn't realized nourished me, especially in the bleary newborn phase. I hadn't known quite what my work meant to me until it was seemingly disappearing.

It was challenging. I once had resolute and concrete expectations of what our family life would look like at this phase, and when I realized I had overshot the mark, I had to reckon with the frustration and disappointment that my dreams and my reality might not match. I wondered if something was wrong with me, that I had this perfect baby girl staring up at me, and yet I yearned to grab my laptop and write, and think, and read. If that seems shallow, trust me, it felt like it. Racked with guilt, I went to Trent and explained. Once I did, we started to slowly reroute our trajectory.

Now, I won't say it was a smooth transition. Even though he supported me wholeheartedly, it took many months and years of juggling and shuffling and reprioritizing to make our schedules work in sync. In truth, it's a constant work in progress as each of our careers and the needs at home shift seasonally. It fluctuates with every move, every switch in school or childcare situation, every job change, even every freelance project I take on. It requires sacrifice and communication and humility, but those are gifts that Trent pours out readily and repeatedly.

And I hope my husband has felt that freedom too. As he has mulled over the pros and cons of a military career and a civilian one, I pray he has never felt beholden to the inclinations of the twenty-two-year-old version of himself who first stepped into a jet. Or the eighteen-year-old one who joined ROTC. At least not on my behalf. I think he knows that whether he should ask to quit tomorrow or stay until retirement, I'd have his six. (This is my only attempt at pilot speak, I promise.)

And maybe that's part of where some modern marriages go wrong. For so many, marriage is a contract. You sign on to a list of prescribed terms, but with the mindset that if something else comes up, or the person changes, or there's a breach of the initial agreement, the contract is null. It is all too easy to dissolve a union. And truthfully, there are times when that off-ramp is an attractive option, especially when it feels like we're running up against situations we did not expect or agree to.

But that's not a Catholic marriage. We believe we enter into not an agreement but a covenant, or a holy union not only between two people but between two people and God. As we read in Ecclesiastes (4:12), "A cord of three strands is not quickly broken." Standing on that altar, it is not the priest who bestows the sacrament but the bride and groom. They stand there and profess they will love the other person the way God loves them, or as close to that love as they can humanly imitate. And in so doing, they will individually and together grow closer to God, because love is of God—because God *is* love (1 John 4:16).

Our marital love is meant to be the strongest, purest version of God's love. It requires the turning of many a cheek (Matthew 5:39), forgiveness well more than seventy-seven times (Matthew 18:22), and humility that runs deep enough that we are willing to give ourselves up for our partner (Ephesians 5:25). It is a truly radical kind of love, one that is all-forgiving, all-understanding, all-changing, all-giving. Or, as is so nicely summed up in Paul's letter to the Corinthians with which we started this chapter, "Love is patient, love is kind. It does not envy, it does not boast, it is not proud. It does not dishonor others, it is not self-seeking, it is not easily angered, it keeps no record of wrongs. Love does not delight in evil but rejoices with the truth. It always protects, always trusts, always hopes, always perseveres. Love never fails" (1 Corinthians 13:4–8).

Or that is what the love given to us by God is meant to be.

For me, I know my love is rarely patient. I am not always kind. And whew, the easily angered bit hits home. In short: I am a delight. But I'm working on changing, on moving toward God's love and away from my weak attempts at human love, with help from my husband. And vice versa. We're slowly, gently, patiently nudging each other toward heaven. Not by force or persuasion, but by loving more and more and more generously. That, I suspect, is how we genuinely change.

As I reflected more, that opportunity to change who you are, to change your mind or even your life, is so very important in military life. We are routinely exposed to new people, new situations, new lifestyles, new cultures, new obstacles, new joys, and so it only follows that if we are open to all these new experiences, if we are authentically plunging into these seasons and scenarios, we must adjust, we must improve, we must grow as we learn.

It's true that all these moving parts make our lives uniquely complicated, but each one has indelibly shaped us. With each move, with each job, with each shift and adjustment and rearrangement, so too have we been altered, hopefully into a purer, truer, more authentic version of ourselves. We are not the people we once were, nor is our marriage what it once was—and this is one of the hidden gifts of military life with all its transitions: we are always examining our priorities and have many opportunities to shape and reshape our life together.

We've witnessed many marriages, especially among our military friends of varying ages and stages, and they have all been a source of wisdom from which we've learned and borrowed and adopted. I think of a commander and his wife who exuded pure fun, joy, and hospitality. Or a couple from church who best modeled to us faith and devotion. Or friends from a brief assignment who showed us what it meant to be open—to kids, to friends, to opportunities, to whims. We have borrowed and patchworked a marriage based on those models, and the pattern we've developed is so very different from what we could have imagined a decade ago—and so much more beautiful. And it's still shifting.

Yes, in so many ways, I am not the woman to whom my husband offered a ring a decade ago. Nor is he the same. And thus, our marriage has dramatically changed from what we envisioned many years and children and experiences prior. I'll venture to guess it will also be different, and hopefully better, a decade from now. In some ways it is hard and seemingly unfair that we are bound to a person who is different from the person we began with. It's also seemingly unfair that our vision of what marriage would be, and what it actually is, evolves too. But the hope is that we are growing *together* as we accompany one another on a lifelong pilgrimage toward heaven. Toward God. Toward that which is always the same, always good, always true.

Now here's the fun part: we get to help each other chart that course. Together, we can envision and dream and work toward our final, holy destination. I hope in ten years we are better at communicating our needs. I hope we're quicker to forgive and slower to anger. I hope patience and presence and trust take deeper root. I hope our love is stronger, richer, fuller for all we experience together. I hope that through repeated attempts at humility, we learn to truly humble ourselves to serve one another. I hope that trust and hope and perseverance become instinctual. I hope that in ten years we see a clearer reflection of Christ in the way we love, the way we serve, the way we live.

When I think back to those fresh-faced twentysomethings standing at the altar a decade ago, there was so much we didn't know. So much we couldn't have known. There were so many people, places, and experiences that entered our path that we couldn't have foreseen. I'm sure our future will hold still yet unknown treasures and trials.

Through it all, I hope we continue to change—together.

Questions for Reflection

1. Go back to the readings and gospel you selected for your marriage ceremony. Why did you choose those readings?
2. What did you promise your spouse on your wedding day? (Feel free to Google the traditional Catholic wedding vows if you need a reminder.) In practice, how has living out those vows shifted over time?
3. Back in chapter 1 we discussed identity. Did marriage shift your concept of your identity? And if so, how?

4. If we return to the idea that our lives involve a lot of change, what milestones—military or otherwise—altered the course of your marriage?
5. How do you envision your marriage will continue to evolve? What do you hope remains the same?
6. In Hebrews 13:8, we read: "Jesus Christ is the same yesterday and today and forever." And in James 1:17, it says: "Every good and perfect gift is from above, coming down from the Father of the heavenly lights, who does not change like shifting shadows." In light of this discussion on change, how can you draw on the immovability and constancy of your faith?

Ξ Chapter 3

FRIENDSHIP + SAINTHOOD

You would not believe how much my heart was strengthened by our resolutions and by everything that contributed to their establishment. I feel an extraordinary sweetness about them as likewise I feel for the love I bear you. Because I love that love incomparably. It is strong, resilient, measureless and unreserved yet gentle, pliant, completely pure and tranquil. In short, if I am not deceived, it is completely in God.

—St. Francis de Sales in a letter to
St. Jane Frances de Chantal

What a wonderful thing it is for two souls to understand each other, for they neither lack something to say, nor grow tired.

—St. Teresa of Ávila, on her friendship
with St. John of the Cross

St. Ignatius of Loyola and St. Francis Xavier
St. Paul and St. Barnabas
St. Felicity and St. Perpetua
St. Teresa of Ávila and St. John of the Cross
St. Brigid and St. Patrick
St. Thomas Aquinas and St. Bonaventure

St. Thérèse of Lisieux and St. Theophane Venard
St. Vincent de Paul and St. Louise de Marillac
St. Jordan of Saxony and St. Diana D'Andalo
St. Martin de Porres and St. Rose of Lima
. . . and the list goes on.

These saintly pairs—who were friends, roommates, pen pals, along with countless others who were siblings (looking at you, Benedict and Scholastica), or parent-child (like Monica and Augustine), or families (notably the Lisieuxs: Louis, Zélie, Thérèse, and servant of God Léonie)—not only knew each other, but influenced one another, and enjoyed genuine friendship. When we see how long the list of these saintly pairs and groups is, it's worth pausing to think about the role of companionship in our search for holiness.

Is it possible that the road to sainthood is easier, more navigable, or even more fun with a friend?

It makes sense. From the jump, Jesus sent his apostles out *in pairs* (Mark 6:7) to evangelize, to shepherd, to heal, to love. Or, even further back, God made Eve because "it is not good for man to be alone" (Genesis 2:18). So it makes sense that God would use the context of relationships to make saints. And if friendship is one of God's favorite methods, we should be on the lookout for him in the people we know and love.

That's all to say this: our desire for friendship is part of our divine design. Perhaps our path to sainthood is best walked with others. As Pope Francis so concisely put it: "Growth in holiness is a journey in community, side by side with others" (*Gaudete et Exsultate* [*Rejoice and Be Glad*], 141).

Even if you consider yourself a lone wolf or an introvert, or you gravitate toward a monk-like solitude, loneliness is a hard cross to bear in this already challenging military lifestyle.

Let me share an example: Fresh into my husband's first operational assignment as an F-15 pilot, he went to Las Vegas for the first of many (truly so, so many) TDYs (for our non-military readers, these are "temporary duty assignments," or work trips). I was among the youngest spouses in the squadron, had no kids, was working remotely, and had a chip on my shoulder about, well, all of it. I wasn't sure if I fit in. I wasn't sure if I *wanted* to fit in. I feared I was among a group of ladies who had lost their drive and were content to keep home and follow their husbands. It was not my most charitable mindset.

While Trent was gone, I came down with severe stomach pains. I had started a friendship with a neighbor, and after a shopping trip to Target, I asked her if we could pop by urgent care. The brusque physician's assistant sent me home with word to ride out whatever stomach bug was after me.

A few hours later, in the middle of the night, I couldn't roll over in bed. The knife-like pains in my abdomen had me pinned flat, while my spine twitched and I dry-heaved. Like any self-respecting grown-up, I called my mom, who happens to be a nurse and demanded I get myself to the emergency room. I drove the few miles on an empty highway and checked myself into the nearest ER, where I was whisked into a room to prep for a series of tests—ultrasound, CAT scan, blood work. While waiting, I realized I should tell someone I was at the hospital. Because of the time zones and flying schedules, Trent was hours behind me and asleep. I didn't want to wake anyone, but there was a key spouse in our squadron who had an infant and, I reckoned, might be awake soon and see my text. I'm sure I texted something very noncommittal like, "Hey, just so someone knows, I'm at the ER. No big deal, just getting some tests done. Might be my appendix or might be nothing. I'll keep you posted."

It was indeed my appendix, but before I could even get wheeled back for surgery, that friend was sitting next to me, both her kids in tow, holding my hand and praying with me. That day, without me asking, a roster of other squadron spouses rotated in and out of the ER so I wasn't alone. They also coordinated to get my husband home, broke into my house (though the details of how have never been revealed!) to pack me a hospital bag, filled our refrigerator with meals and groceries, and brought me magazines, books, and activities for the weeks of recovery that would follow. It was, frankly, astounding. People who did not know me—some who had never even met me—stepped up to care for me.

That may have been the first time I was carried by generous companionship, but it was not the last. I have been welcomed to so many families' dinner tables. Rubbermaid bins filled with secondhand clothes magically appear on my porch when my children grow into the next size. People have scouted and toured homes for us when we were committing to housing from afar. There are people flung across the globe who cheer on my accomplishments, who pray for my sorrows or worries, who motivate me by their generosity, their patience, their resilience, and their examples of faithfulness, of service, of parenthood, of womanhood. There are bits and pieces I admire and try to emulate in each of these companions. They are not perfect, but they are my saints on Earth, lighting the path for me to follow.

Another story: Even before the appendix debacle, within days of arriving on base, I was welcomed in by a woman who had three children and was pregnant with her fourth. Her house was loud and chaotic, but she always had an open door. As I would jog or walk past, her front door was nearly always ajar, welcoming whoever might pass by. I too like to host, but

I like to host when my house has been freshly cleaned, when there are baked goods being pulled from the oven, when there is a hot pot of coffee. In sum, I like to show love when I'm good and ready and very, very prepared. But that's not true love or true charity. My friend, on the other hand, is always ready to serve and love others, regardless of what else is brewing in the background.

The point here is that true friendship can take many different forms. What serves one friend well may not serve another. And if we are to pour our love into them, we ought to be open to how we love them.

I, for example, like to talk to friends on the phone. I want to know the intricacies of their day-to-day lives, what is energizing them, what is troubling them, what they're making for dinner. I have friends who prefer to keep in touch via text, or in one case, via Instagram memes and reels. It's perhaps not my most natural way of connecting, but to maintain that friendship, I've had to open myself to that option, albeit in my own way, with dialogue attached.

I believe St. Francis de Sales and St. Jane Frances de Chantal had radical openness to unexpected friendship. She was a widow, lost in grief for her beloved spouse. She had prayed to find someone to help her navigate her new and lonely world. He was a young bishop and a skilled writer and preacher. She requested he serve as her spiritual director, and after some hesitation he agreed. The friendship quickly bloomed.

Together, they founded the Order of the Visitation in Annecy, France. The order accepted older women who were not well suited to the more rigorous practices of other orders and, instead, encouraged them to develop a prayer life and to emulate Mary's little virtues of humility, obedience, poverty, charity, and patience. In short, the sisters sought to emulate the virtues that Mary displayed in journey to her cousin Elizabeth in the Visitation. What began as a modest congregation resulted in eighty-six foundations by the time Jane died. Today there are more than one hundred monasteries around the globe. The order also boasts seven martyrs and several open causes for canonization, including Sr. "Léonie" Françoise-Thérèse Martin, the sister of the beloved St. Thérèse of Lisieux.

The relationship between Jane and Francis also nuanced our understanding of the role of love and friendship in Christian spirituality. Because of their connection, Francis was able to describe in his book *Introduction to the Devout Life* how pure and true friendships are both of God and lead people to God: "If the bond of your mutual liking be charity, devotion and Christian perfection, God knows how very precious a friendship it is! Precious because it comes from God, because it tends to God, because God is the link that binds you, because it will last for ever in him. Truly it is a blessed thing to love on earth as we hope to love in heaven, and to begin that friendship here which is to endure for ever there."

So where do we, who are not part of a religious order, find those friends—people rooted in charity, devotion, and perfection? Perhaps by becoming such a friend ourselves.

We can learn to be generous: Volunteer to make a meal for a new mom. When you drop it off, bring her a coffee, too, or offer to watch the baby while she hops in the shower. Follow up a few weeks later, once the crowds have oohed and aahed at the new babe and then disappeared. That's when she may need you most.

We can learn to be vulnerable: Invite someone over for coffee. Set up a playdate. Offer to get a beer after work. Start a book club—with this book as your launching point! It is so very awkward to put yourself out there like this, and some people will tell you no. Keep trying.

We can learn to be hospitable: After church, introduce yourself to a new family. Offer to have them over for donuts the following week.

We can learn to be authentic: Attend a squadron, group, or base event. Join people for a reading group, trivia night, wine tasting, axe throwing, painting, hang gliding, whatever the Marines do for fun. If it's something you're interested in, chances are, you'll meet people who share your interests.

We can learn to love: Find a little something you like in someone who is already nearby, and build from there. They do not need to be a saint. They do not need to be perfect. Not all friendships will stick. Not all friendships will grow. Some friendships may even be painful. Cast a wide net and look for virtue. Look for people who do not gossip, who extend hospitality generously, who are kind and authentic, who love freely and want the best for you.

We can learn to relearn. We change with seasons, with locations, with the needs of our families—our friendship needs may shift as well. Where we once needed someone fun and silly to pull us out of our shell, now we may need reliability or steadiness. Apply some self-knowledge to find the types of friendships that will nourish us, not drain us.

We can learn to be open. Sometimes our richest relationships are with those who are in a very different phase of life. The priest who celebrated our wedding is among my favorite dinner companions—he is in his eighties. Before I had children, I loved snuggling friends' babies while they had a rare night out. We have long had an open-door policy for a home-cooked meal to all the bachelors in my husband's squadron. Our friends do not necessarily need to be similar to us—St.

Jane Frances de Chantal was fiery; St. Francis de Sales was even-keeled.

Our family is in a new friendship phase now. We just moved to a new base, one where we don't have an existing social network. It is so challenging to find my people—but it is worth the discomfort and intentionality to find the *right* people.

We need friends who know us truly, deeply, authentically. Our friendships don't need to be fancy. They can be full of sweatpants and teary eyes during a deployment. Wine and Ritz crackers while the kids sleep. Lukewarm coffee in a thermos while pushing a swing. A coveted double-date night. We need people who know our dreams and goals and fears, people who push, encourage, love, challenge, enrich, and inspire us. Above all, we need people to nudge us along on our pilgrimage to eternity.

It may take time, but those people—the Teresa to our John, the Brigid to our Patrick, the Francis Xavier to our Ignatius—are out there. We just need to find them.

Questions for Reflection

1. Think of the friendships you most cherish. What is it about those particular relationships that make them rich?
2. Are there relationships that drain you? Why might that be?
3. Who are the people in your network whom you'd like to befriend? Where would you find places to meet those friends? How could you make those aspirations reality?

4. What are the wedges or challenges that make new friendships difficult in military life?
5. How has your experience of community and friendship impacted your journey?
6. Which friendships in the Bible stand out to you? What speaks to you about these relationships?

Ξ Chapter 4

TDY + CONSISTENCY

> Priest: Pray, brothers and sisters, that my sacrifice and yours may be acceptable to God, the almighty Father.
>
> Congregation: May the Lord accept the sacrifice at your hands for the praise and glory of his name, for our good and the good of all his holy Church.
>
> —Order of Mass, Preparatory Rite

Late in 2015, Trent arrived at his first operational assignment. The squadron had just returned from a deployment. They were tired. Half the squadron spouses were pregnant. And then they got a new influx of young lieutenants, or as they sarcastically referred to themselves, COGS (like cogs in a wheel), who were frothing at the mouth to be full-up fighter pilots. Frothing with excitement quickly turned to frothing with frustration as they clocked in some two-hundred-plus days of TDYs, a few HUREVACs (a process to evacuate the jets, *but not the families*, when a hurricane approaches), and a six-month-plus deployment—all in the course of three years. The pace was dizzying, and I'm sure many of you reading this have endured even worse.

Deployments I was prepared for. When you sign up to marry someone in the military, that is always the dark-but-known cloud overhead. But the TDY tempo was an unfortunate revelation, one of many surprises in this lifestyle. And one that was jarring.

He'd be gone for three weeks, home for two, gone again for two. Lather, rinse, repeat. The locations and time zones changed. The number of days gone and home were always in flux. He rarely actually came home the day he was meant to, so the return was an estimate, with plus or (rarely/never) minus four days built into my mental calendar. It felt that the minute we got into a routine, he'd leave. When I'd get into a solo routine, he'd suddenly be at the front door. It was a constant state of whiplash and readjustment.

Years later, the inconsistency of TDYs still means living in a state of chronic adjustment for the whole family: the dance of home and away, fluctuating routines, and massaged rules when Dad is home versus gone. And while the departures are for valuable, necessary causes, it can be hard on the home front.

During that bleary time as a fresh military spouse, I remember a command spouse sharing with us that she served dinner at 5:30, every night, no matter what. She said she did not care if her husband was flying, in a meeting, on a deployment, or in the shower, dinner was on the table to give her kids predictability, when so much of their life was not. The same went for bedtime. The family kept a schedule, and he was welcome to pop in and out of that routine as he could. At the time, I remember that seeming so rigid, as I flexed and molded my schedule to fit Trent's. But now, with two kids, I realize that routine is a valuable antidote to chaos. We've since adopted similar habits that allow us to keep a constant rhythm at home, despite whatever is happening at work or otherwise.

Now, maintaining this rhythm means I need to be able to do it all myself. That means everything from prepping dinner to getting the kids ready for school to planning our social calendar and holidays—it all needs to be able to be done solo, because it often *is* done solo.

That's a hard pill to swallow for both parties. I imagine it's hard for active-duty service members to accept that your family has a routine and you're semi-external to that routine. I'm sure it doesn't feel good to feel like you're an optional sub on the bench of your family's team. We have periods where that is evident in our life—when roles become awkward, like when the kids insist on Mom for bedtime and bathtime and books, even when Dad is home, because that feels more normal. Or when he returns and they no longer eat a certain food, or they like something done a special way, and he just isn't aware. That feeling of being an outsider can be a real wound, and openly discussing it and addressing it where you can is so important.

On the other hand, there are times the bulk of our life falls to me. In addition to my own laundry list of tasks, I have to clumsily grab ahold of one of his home responsibilities while he's away, like properly tying the trash bags shut or turning on the backyard grill, and I might not feel confident in how I complete those tasks. I may even have moments of resentment that the life *we* built is often *mine* to maintain.

One of those solo responsibilities is gathering our family for Mass attendance, which once struck fear in my heart as I pushed my two tots into a pew and prayed for silence. But now, I'm not so intimidated.

See, I've learned to look to the ritual of Mass as something of a comfort, especially when my husband is gone. Much of that is being in the presence of Jesus, being in the presence of other families, other believers, other sinners, other trying-their-bests. But there's something to be said for the routine pace of the Mass itself.

We are greeted with the same welcome every week; we recite the same creed; we always hear two readings, a psalm, a gospel. Every week, we gather around the altar for the same breaking of bread and pouring of wine. We walk up the same aisle in the same procession to receive Jesus's presence in Communion. We know when to sit, when to stand, when to kneel, when to listen for a call, and when and what to respond.

If that sounds rote, it can be. But it can also be richly welcoming. In many ways, it's choreography that you never forget, that you can join in whenever and wherever you are. Whether we attend Mass in Connecticut or Korea or an aircraft carrier floating in the ocean, there is a predictability—a stability to what we experience, to how we worship God. And that can be awfully comforting when little else in our life is consistent.

What's more, no matter where in the world you celebrate Mass, the readings are the same. A Protestant milspouse friend once mentioned to me how amazing it was that the readings I heard while doling out Cheerios in North Carolina are the same that Trent heard while in a Vegas chapel, and our parents and siblings heard wherever they were. It was something I had taken for granted, but it's true that the universality of the Catholic Church allows for a shared experience, a familiar experience, and a welcoming experience, no matter where you find yourself. It also gives space to grow and share faith with others, even while apart. On separated Sundays, Trent and I often share the takeaways from the homilies at our different Masses, knowing we both heard the same readings but may have gathered different gems from the discussion. It gives us a way to share in worship, even if we can't physically be together.

And because our Mass is familiar, I admit there are times it all blurs together. There are times I zone out and miss the beauty and intent of each little line, each gesture, each moment. But look back at the prayer at the beginning of this chapter—the exchange we have with the presider after we've brought our gifts to the altar, which you've likely heard hundreds of times before. It occurs after the offertory while shoes scuff and kneelers bang and people groan as they stand up as we prepare for the Liturgy of the Eucharist. This prayer speaks of sacrifice. Yes, it references the bread and blood that are broken and poured out for us. It references the way we bring our own resources to worship with the money we drop into the collection baskets. And it also reminds us of the little sacrifices we bring with us to Mass to unite with Jesus's sacrifice.

While our partners rush into the line of duty, whether on TDY or deployment or daily life, we're there, tending children, tending house, tending a life left behind. We do groceries and fill out permission slips and tuck tired children into bed after rushing them from school to soccer while tossing French fries into the backseat. We sign both our names to birthday cards and condolence notes. We watch weather radars and worry and kill the car battery. We herd our wild sheep to Mass and try to maintain peace. Still, our actions can feel so small and so insignificant. But we can offer them to Jesus, and suddenly they gain significance.

Finding the significance in those small, daily sacrifices has paid off in our life in surprising ways. Instead of wearing us down, I can find meaning in them because they become avenues for prayerful connection to Jesus—and that has sustained me for the long haul. We're now in a season where I travel some. And because we've discovered meaning in attending to the details of hand-offs and briefings on kiddie and home needs, the coming and going has become seamless, regardless of who is leaving. We better appreciate now that neither the traveler nor the at-homer has it easy, so we can approach both roles with greater empathy. Those challenging years of establishing routines, learning each other's roles, and understanding our children's reactions have in many ways paid off.

In one of my recent travels, I took a moms' getaway with a few of our closest friends from our first assignment. The women in this group had been flung to every corner of the country, so the reunion was joyful. We joked the time away was our payback for all those repeat TDYs from years ago. Over cupcakes and wine, we reminisced on that period. We remembered the chaos, the disorientation, the exasperation. And not one of us, given the choice, would erase it.

TDYs taught us what we were made of. It revealed to us who had our backs. It was a blazing crucible that forged friendships that have endured time and distance, peaks and valleys. We shared meals, celebrated holidays, bonded over heartache and tears, and cheered each other on. We watched each other become stronger, wiser, gentler, smarter, and, perhaps above all, more confident. And the same went for our active-duty husbands. Being road warriors brought them together over work, over meals, over bedbug-infested hotel rooms, over shenanigans, over missed milestones back home, over stress. These are our forever friends because we have all done something hard together.

Now, community isn't always the silver lining with TDYs. My husband has a new role that requires travel, only without the camaraderie and support we both enjoyed in his operational assignment. We're looking for new joys in this new trial. When he's gone, I binge the crappy television shows he would never agree to watch, make breakfast for dinner on repeat, and stay up late working or reading or just thinking. He eats sushi and goes running early in the morning and heads to bed way earlier than I would ever condone. We've found that now, in a life of routine, a little bit of freedom is reenergizing.

That freedom can mean enriching ourselves in new ways. In between bouts of moping and complaining, I reignited an old love of photography. I became yoga certified. I've asked new people over to our home for coffee. The kids and I have traveled. We've had Happy Meal picnics on the living room floor or sleepovers in our master bedroom. We intentionally build something to look forward to into each TDY, even if something small. And we find time for God. We ask God what he is asking of us during this time. I schlep the kids to Mass, even if it's hard and we're late or I forget money for the collection, all in order to give thanks and ask for strength to carry on. That rhythm of worship keeps us centered because it brings meaning to our sacrifices—it's like a beating heart, drawing us in and sending us out every week.

That brief, weekly Mass attendance itself offers us a chance to root ourselves in something bigger, something better, than inconsistency and frustration. It gives us routine and a guidepost in our week, and, I hope, sends the message to my children that nothing is more important than our time with God. In turn, that regular attendance allows us to better live out the liturgical seasons, which, I've realized, contain natural countdowns in the Church not unlike the ones we keep in the military. There are long spells of ordinary time; there are hopeful celebrations during Pentecost, Christmas, and Easter; periods to reflect and wait during Advent and Lent. There are days of thanksgiving, of adoration, of awe, of penitence, of grief. And if as Christians, we really believe Jesus is going to return, aren't we waiting for him through it all?

Is it possible that as we wait with our children, our homes, our litany of chores during one, two, or twenty TDYs, we're actually learning to wait for Jesus? Are we learning to count down to his presence? To desire his return? And do we appreciate how beautifully and profoundly our faith and military lives can and do intersect?

And so at our house we wait, yes, for Dad to return from yet another TDY, but also for Jesus. The ultimate homecoming.

Questions for Reflection

1. Reflect on your personal TDY tempo. What are the challenges and fruits?
2. What kind of support do you need during TDYs? How might you support others whose spouses are TDY?
3. Reflect on the themes of inconsistency and stability. Where do you see each manifest in your own life? Are there any changes you'd like to make?
4. What parts of Mass nourish you? What are the challenges of sustaining a regular rhythm of worship?
5. How can you tap into offerings and ministries from your parish to find support? What might you be able to offer others facing a TDY if you are in a stable season of life?

6. Are there any phrases or actions from Mass that are jumping out to you in a new way recently? Anything that allows you to sink deeper into the mystery of the Mass or into the reality of military life?

Ξ Chapter 5

PARENTING + KNOWING JESUS

> The family is the original cell of social life. It is the natural society in which husband and wife are called to give themselves in love and in the gift of life. Authority, stability, and a life of relationships within the family constitute the foundations for freedom, security, and fraternity within society. The family is the community in which, from childhood, one can learn moral values, begin to honor God, and make good use of freedom. Family life is an initiation into society.
>
> —*Catechism of the Catholic Church,* 2207

> Parents have the first responsibility to the education of their children. They bear witness to this responsibility first by creating a home where tenderness, forgiveness, respect, fidelity, and disinterested service are the rule. The home is well suited for the education in the virtues.
>
> —*Catechism of the Catholic Church,* 2223

Harken back to your life before children. Even before marriage if it suits you. I want you to call to mind what you thought parenthood would be like. Did you think of having soft, doughy babies cooing gently in a bassinet? A toddler running a choo-choo around the carpet? Or maybe a teenager with whom you shoot hoops?

Now let me take you to a scene in my real life: We were in Ireland for my sister's wedding, which yes, was even more beautiful than you are envisioning. My sweet little flower girl, in the absence of a nap and several time zones out of her norm, started crying midway through the ceremony and refused to be in many of the bridal party photos. Just an hour later, her kilt-clad brother was also frustrated by the state of his toddlerdom and threw a fit so dramatic that he managed to dislocate his elbow. Thankfully, Papa spent his career in orthopedics, so after his father-of-the-bride speech he managed to pop it back in so the ring bearer could hit the dance floor.

The photos from this destination event show none of this chaos, however. From the photo reel of green hills, misty beaches, and smiling faces, it looks like perfection.

Real life and fantasy don't always align. We know they rarely do. The problem is that everywhere—from our social media feeds, to our quick chats with other parents at the playground, to glancing around at the other clean and well-behaved families at Mass—fantasy is depicted as reality. The women in our social media feed have clean homes. Their kids' meals are homemade, perhaps cut into cutesy little shapes before being delicately organized into a bento box. They have a monthly family photo in a pumpkin patch. And while building a snowman. And chasing leprechauns in a field of four-leaf clovers while rainbows streak across the sky. Or something like that.

Jokes aside, despite the pressure we put on ourselves, we are not called to make our family lives a fantasy.

To make sure that I could brazenly make that claim, I read a lot of the *Catechism*—basically all of it that reckons with parenthood, families, and children. There was no mention of Instagram-worthy parenting—not breastfeeding or baby-led weaning or Montessori methods or crying it out or potty training or classical education or gentle parenting. None of these approaches are required by the Church. Our Christian faith does not stipulate that you throw your child a hand-crafted birthday party, take them to a waterpark every summer, or shape their pancakes into reindeer or snowmen or hearts. It does not even stipulate how you raise your kids as a stay-at-home parent or a working parent or as a combination of the two. And I believe that's intentional. If we are to truly live in the gifts and vocations that God has specially given to us as individuals, it's important that the framework is loose to accommodate the many ways we all parent.

Now none of those activities are inherently wrong. Many are the foundations of memories and joy and wonder with our children. Some might even bring us joy. The problem arises if we're only doing them because we feel we *ought* to, or because we're trying to fit a particular, perhaps idealistic, mold of parenthood, or because we believe parenthood is a painful dying to self for the miniature authoritarians who smear things on our walls and lick our windowpanes. Somewhere along the way martyrdom and parenthood have gotten conflated, and we've not-so-subtly taught a generation of moms and dads they are meant to give all—not for Christ, but for their children.

Yes, part of our vocation as parents is to unstick that pesky selfishness deep within us, but we are not meant to hand it over to our children so they can have free rein. Instead, our dying to self is about reorienting ourselves to Christ. Our children undoubtedly help us on that journey. They give us the opportunity to practice patience and grace and humility and forgiveness and joy and wonder. But they are not the end goal. Giving them, and ourselves, to Jesus is.

So what does Jesus and the Church require of us as parents? It's actually a pretty short list:

1. Love (*CCC*, 2207)
2. Teaching your children to love God, and be obedient to God (*CCC*, 2222)
3. Attending to your children's moral education and spiritual formation (*CCC*, 2221 and 2226)
4. Respect, of all parties, by all parties (*CCC*, 2222)

The brevity here is especially important for military families. Some of you might be overseas and wondering if you're neglecting your children by being absent. Others may be dealing with a dearth of resources. You may be single-parenting during a deployment. You may not have a grandparent or aunt or uncle who can pop by so you can Christmas shop for an afternoon. Even a trip to the playground may just feel like too much after a week of stress, especially if you don't have a friend to go with. Consider this your reminder that if it does not bring you or your child closer to God, then you can let it go.

And I've been here. As I mentioned earlier, in my earliest days of motherhood I wrestled with my self-imposed expectation that I would be a stay-at-home mom and the shocking realization that I missed the creativity and stimulation work had provided me. And I realized that when I was depleted, I didn't feel like a very good, present, joyful mother. Yes, I was doing all the things I thought I *should be* doing, but I was doing them begrudgingly, and was that really serving anyone well? In time I came to realize I could better serve my family if I also, simultaneously, attended to my own needs—and embraced my own primary vocation as a daughter of God first, a wife second, and only then, third, a mother. And so I outsourced part-time childcare, bulked up my workload, hustled to find new clients, wrote essays that were percolating in my heart, snuck in some lunch-dates with my husband, and meanwhile became a happier, healthier, more present mother. And still there are days—like when I drop my kids off to summer school and realize the parking lot is empty and their classes are smaller because many parents are staying at home with them for the summer—when I am overcome with unbearable guilt. I wonder if I'm serving them properly, living in my vocation to motherhood in the fullest way, or if I've taken the selfish path.

But then I think about the women in my life I most admire and respect. Each has carved a unique fulfillment of the term motherhood. Some work out of the house full time. Some volunteer. Some bask in the authentic joy of nurturing, educating, feeding little ones. But the ones who live in a way tailored to them are typically the most content.

And if we're still not convinced of the uniqueness of each motherhood, we can consider the saints. St. Zélie Martin was a lacemaker while attending to the souls of her saints-to-be. St. Gianna Beretta Molla was a doctor. St. Monica campaigned relentlessly for her son Augustine's conversion. St. Elizabeth Ann Seton became a nun *after* raising her five children. St. Anne spent most of her years barren until she finally conceived Mary. Their paths to and embodiments of motherhood are wildly different, so if we have guilted and convinced ourselves today that ours ought to all be similar, we have erred.

And, I realized, if I'm wallowing in my own guilt, then I'm probably not focusing on what's truly important: bringing my family closer to God. So too, if I'm preoccupied with the parenting fluff I feel I ought to be doing, I might avoid the deeper, more important task of helping my children grow not just in obedience and respect for God but in genuine love for God. As my kids became toddlers with their own opinions and questions, I found myself pondering how to do this effectively, and so I went to a lecture on it. The mothers' group at my church invited another parishioner with expertise in catechesis and mothering to speak to us. She had many valuable insights, such as the value of praying for the specific needs of our children, such as their acne or dealing with a bully—even if those things seem insignificant. But her number one piece of advice really stuck with me: teach your children that Jesus is real.

Not a week before this, as we drove in the car, my four-year-old piped up from the backseat:

Four-year-old: "Is Jesus real?"

Me: "What? Yes! Of course!" And then, under my breath, "What do you think we're doing at church every week?!"

Four-year-old: "Is the Grinch real?"

Me: "No."

Four-year-old: "Are ducks real?"

Me: "Are you kidding?"

She was not kidding. As I ruminated on how the Grinch, Jesus, and ducks all could possibly fall in the same gray category for her, it started to make sense. Our children are told hundreds of stories when they're small—for good reason! It's a great way to teach them and entertain them and foster imagination, wonder, morality, and more. But because we don't contextualize these stories when we sit down to read

Goldilocks and the Three Bears or the Gospel of Luke, it probably is hard for them to sift through what is make-believe (that bears cannot talk and do not eat porridge) and what is real (that Jesus raised people from the dead). In reflection, they do seem similarly unbelievable. So much of our faith borders on the implausible, even for our adult sensibilities.

When the speaker from our parish talked about helping our children encounter Jesus as a living person who is truly present to us in our daily experience, it clicked. I had to make sure my children knew we imitate and praise him as a person who walks with us to bring us the fullness of God's love.

Then the trick becomes how to do that in an age-appropriate manner. For my young toddlers, we've converted the contents of our church bag to religious toys: play nativities, dolls of Mary and Joseph, religious books. We've started an evening devotional for preschoolers. Before Mass on Sundays, we talk about how we get dressed up because we love Jesus and we're going to see him. We have even ventured into Adoration a time or two, which they adorably call "quick church," so they can both see their parents praying and quietly ask questions they may be too sheepish to ask during Mass. These actions are but small seeds that I hope someday will bloom into their own, personal relationship with Jesus.

And that is our call as parents: to plant the love of Christ somewhere in our kids—through stories, through prayer, through Mass participation and plenty of explanations, through modeling virtue, through our own joy, through whatever means necessary—so that when the time comes, they know, love, and serve him.

Those seeds may take time to grow, or they might quickly spring up. My daughter's faith has quickly taken root. One Sunday, while sitting next to a depiction of the crowning of thorns, she spewed a series of thoughtful questions at us in whispers: "Did the crown of thorns make Jesus bleed?" "Did they take it off him when they put him on the Cross?" "Was Jesus mean to the people who hurt him when he came back?"

Just as I basked in all I had done right to nurture that faith, I went up to receive Communion while holding my son's hand. As I took the Body of Christ, he turned to me, and not so quietly asked, "Did that man give you a cucumber?!" And just like that, I was re-humbled.

But just as I assumed my three-year-old son was absorbing way less than his sister, one morning I overheard him singing in his room while playing trucks. He sang: "Jesus died on Earth! Jesus took his clothes off and then he died because the bad guys were so rude! But he came back. He died on Earth. The bad guys didn't have words."

His little ditty is theologically sound, though there are some odd details we'll smooth over when he's older. Still, it's amazing what children absorb, what they latch onto, and what moves them. And we don't have to be a theologian to present it to them. We just need time and repetition and honesty as we share our own faith with them.

As I navigate it all, I come back to the beginning of this chapter. To nurture my children well, I had to start saying no to the things that were clouding my version of authentic parenthood. I don't like Halloween, so we nixed pumpkin carving and driving for an hour to go to the pumpkin patch. I cut my Christmas shopping in half, which allowed me time to bake cookies and scones and brittles and thematic pancakes, over which my children screamed with delight. Instead of belaboring over Christmas craft ideas from Instagram (which I routinely and comically mess up), I bought craft packages at Hobby Lobby. We used photos from our year of travels instead of a holiday photo shoot. I said no to social media by deleting it off my phone, and suddenly became a little more present and a little less agitated with my kids.

Each humble, little no allowed me to say a wholehearted yes. It has allowed me to delight in them, to wonder with them, to find awe and curiosity anew, in relation both to God and to daily life. Nurturing those feelings in all of us opens doors to a deeper relationship with God and with each other. Now, we're still busy, and there's no end to that in sight, but being busy with the things that enrich, improve, and sustain us feels like richer soil to tend faith in.

Questions for Reflection

1. Examine your notions of what you believe you must do as a good Catholic parent. Are they in line with the Church's rather simple teaching? Where are there places you could improve? Where are there other places you could give yourself room to simplify?
2. What practices could you lead for your family to start shifting your children's gaze to Jesus?
3. How can you model an authentic relationship with God, yourself?
4. Reflect on your parenting. What are the habits that you hope impact your children?
5. Where have you treated your parenthood as a martyrdom? How can you reorient those sacrifices to God?
6. How can you carve out some time to spend with your children and Jesus? Some ideas include praying the Rosary, going to Adoration, writing a prayer together,

reading Bible stories, bonding over Christian coloring pages, etc. Share what worked for you with your partner or small group.

Ξ Chapter 6

ASSIGNMENTS + TRUST

> We are all asked if we will surrender what we are, our humanity, our flesh and blood, to the Holy Spirit and allow Christ to fill the emptiness formed by the particular shape of our life. The surrender that is asked of us includes complete and absolute trust; it must be like Our Lady's surrender, without condition and without reservation. . . . What we shall be asked is to give our flesh and blood, our daily life—our thoughts, our service to one another, our affections and loves, our words, our intellect, our waking, working, and sleeping, our ordinary human joys and sorrows—to God. To surrender all that we are, as we are, to the Spirit of Love in order that our lives may bear Christ into the world—that is what we shall be asked.
>
> —Carryl Houselander, *The Reed of God*

My husband jokes that when the time rolls around to rank his preferred locations for our next move, he ought to put his first choice second. Always, without fail, our number-two pick is the assignment he receives.

Comedy aside, second is pretty good, especially as we've seen folks receive assignments they truly did not want or had never heard of. For our non-military readers, let that sink in. Families are told to move across the country or even the world to locations they do not want to go to, and there is little they can do to stop it. Some of those locations are prohibitively expensive. Or so remote that their extended families or friends can't or won't visit. Some placements mean leaving your children behind for months or even more than a year. Some mean embracing schools or houses or communities that are subpar. And this doesn't even touch on the moral dilemma that service members feel when these assignments require their families to make monumental sacrifices in order to make their military service possible. In many ways, the ideal of "service before self," which in itself has ties to our faith, transforms into "service before all" or "service before family," which are suddenly less palatable propositions. And so it makes sense that a lot of military families gripe that the needs of the military almost always outweigh the needs and desires of each family. The past experiences, combined with future what-ifs and fears, can be overwhelming and leave military families with a salty perspective on the mysterious assignment process.

Those challenges are real and true. They require introspection and hard conversations and honesty. The assignment process requires detachment and a sense of adventure and even submission. But after more than a decade riding that wave, we've come to trust we always end up where we're meant to be—where God intends for us to be.

God's providence became abundantly clear as Russian tanks rolled into Ukraine in February 2022. Just a year prior we had requested an assignment to eastern Europe, with Ukraine at the top of our list. I pondered how, given our druthers, we could have been with our toddlers in an active war zone. In that moment I saw so clearly how God had guided us and protected us, even while we kicked and screamed in the back seat.

A similar thing happened during the COVID-19 pandemic. We had requested to be overseas, but after the world shut down, I was so thankful to have family within driving distance, especially when we welcomed our second child and leaned on family support. We may have grumbled about that assignment at the time, but the stability was a true godsend given the state of the world otherwise.

I share this not as a tell-all, but because it's hard to see things clearly in the moment. It's hard not to get what we ask for. Our egos don't like being told that we're not good enough. That our request will not be honored. Or that someone (or even Someone) knows better. My husband and I will readily admit we have not always taken those revelations gracefully. There have been many nights spent griping and whining. Many discussions with friends over what or who is navigating our futures. Many daydreams of what-ifs and what-could-have-beens.

Given my musings on this lack of control, it makes sense that I found resonance between our military life and *The Reed of God* by Carryl Houselander. This classic meditation on Mary was published in the thick of World War II, as people were surrounded by unknowns and fear and anxiety. It is a profoundly beautiful book, with so many snippets that will stop you in your tracks, but one in particular caught my attention. I have always viewed Mary's *fiat,* her yes to the invitation to bring God into the world, as this monumental milestone that forever shaped humanity. And it is that. But Houselander offers another perspective:

"It was so tremendous, yet so passive. She was not asked to do anything herself, but to let something be done to her. She was not asked to renounce anything, but to receive an incredible gift."

Mary's gift, Houselander says, is in so many ways her obedience and her receptivity. Today, we are so motivated by milestones, by actions, by tangible successes. We admire people with drive, with hustle, with innovation. Far less often do we praise the person who is patient, who waits until the right time, who does nothing. But Houselander suggests that Mary's accomplishment was not something she did herself—instead, it was allowing *God* to accomplish something in her. We all have the capacity to allow God to work in us.

Houselander reminds us we are called to surrender, which is not a term military folk are particularly fond of! We must surrender to God's will—to let *his will be done.* To do that, we must release our white-knuckled grasp of the steering wheel, and let God drive while we sit in the passenger seat. We can still offer recommended directions, or an idea for a rest stop or destination we'd like to see, but we're called to ultimately trust his navigation. Just to put things in perspective, Houselander reminds us that "we shall not be asked to do more than the Mother of God."

Rereading the account of the annunciation in the Gospel of Luke, what stuck out to me in a new way is that Gabriel does not ask Mary for permission. He doesn't ask her if she's cool with bearing the Messiah. He doesn't ask her for her opinion. He is not a FedEx agent asking for a signature for the massive delivery that is about to occur in her womb. He simply tells her what is about to happen.

That does not take away from her gracious response. Mary had free will and chose to respond with complete surrender, grace, and trust. She could have said no—she could have even said yes and then stomped her foot and bemoaned her situation all the while. She didn't, and that's important. But so too is Gabriel's language because it reminds us that God does not have to ask permission to act, even if we pretend or plead otherwise. He is sovereign.

The military also doesn't ask permission. Now, let's pause for clarity: I do not mean to equate the military's orders with God's, as they are not the same thing. Let's repeat: God's orders and the military's are not on an even playing field. Got it? Okay, but what if we believed God's providence is active in those manmade orders? And what if we viewed our response to military orders as a practice round in obedience and generosity so we can better respond when God calls? What if we took bad assignments with less gnashing of teeth and with a hopeful demeanor? Or what if we praised God for good assignments? And regardless of the assignment, what if we truly believed, truly trusted, that good would come?

I remember a wing command spouse's shared wisdom for everyone fretting at assignment time: "Bloom where you're planted." Those words have stayed with me through easy assignments and challenging ones, even more so when I learned that this phrase originated from something that St. Francis de Sales is believed to have said: "Truly charity has no limit; for the love of God has been poured into our hearts by his Spirit dwelling in each one of us, calling us to a life of devotion and inviting us to bloom in the garden where he has planted and directing us to radiate the beauty and spread the fragrance of his Providence."

And this is where free will is important. We cannot control where we get sent. We cannot control what the housing market looks like there, or if the schools are underperforming, or if the job will require chronic time away. What we can control is our response to each hurdle. We can choose if we bloom or if we wither. We can control if and how we "radiate beauty" or "spread the fragrance of providence."

There can be good found wherever you go: A house, or even a room, you love. A school where your children flourish. A playground with fond memories. A grocery store stocked just so. A tree that provides shade. Dear friends. An unexpected adventure. A moment of contentment. Lessons learned. A job you believe in. There is always something to be grateful for. There is always a reason to give thanks, and even tiny seeds of thanksgiving can blossom.

And that goes back to the beginning of this story. Hindsight is a powerful tool in helping us understand our past so we can better navigate and understand our future. Time and time again, even when I did not initially believe it, we have found ourselves somewhere fruitful, and I can only believe that God places his hand into the assignment process so we end up where we're meant to be.

We stayed in North Carolina far longer than we ever anticipated or desired. But rooting there allowed us to build a strong base in our family and in our community. The friendships we built over time are among the strongest in our life.

On the flipside, we were amped about an assignment to California. But once the allure of perfect weather, an idyllic campus, and a buzzing restaurant scene died away, we realized just how foreign the culture was to us, and how removed from our community we felt. The back half of our assignment was a slow slog, but it forced us to articulate what was missing, what was important, and what the path forward might look like. That clarity was such a bright takeaway that helped us chart our course.

When our most recent assignment time came up, I finally learned my lesson. My husband and I still had long conversations where we shared our questions, opinions, and concerns. We still weighed pros and cons and tried to forecast.

But when it came time to submit preferences, I felt at peace. I surrendered. I knew we'd end up where we needed to be, and that once we got there, we'd realize what God needed us to do while there.

I think this book is part of that surrender. In our latest assignment, I had pleaded to God for something new, something creative. I was handed time and space and clarity to write. References and connections and even, most surprising, childcare fell into my lap. It seemed as if once I turned on the engine, it went on its own. It was not me, of that I am certain.

Had we landed elsewhere, would it have been the same? Or would I have filled my time otherwise? Would the embered inkling to serve the military families I know and love have burned out?

Perhaps. Or perhaps it would have been something else with its own beauty, but I'm thankful for this. For right now. For being where I needed to be.

Questions for Reflection

1. What assignments have you initially received with frustration, dread, or disbelief? In retrospect, how might God have been leading you in hidden or surprising ways?
2. Look back at the full roster of your assignments and locations. What unexpected good came from each of those? What challenges arrived?
3. How can you better "bloom where you are planted"?
4. How can you personally better practice obedience and surrender? How can you become more receptive to the Lord?

5. Houselander writes, "The remedy for fear is trust in God." How does that speak to the assignment process? Or to other parts of military life? What practices deepen your trust in God?

Ξ Chapter 7

MOVING + PRESENCE

> In the course of their journey, he came to a village where a woman named Martha welcomed him into her home. She had a sister named Mary who sat at the Lord's feet and listened to what he was saying. But Martha was distracted by her many tasks. So she came to him and said, "Lord, do you not care that my sister has left me to do all the work by myself? Tell her to come and help me." The Lord answered her: "Martha, Martha, you are anxious and upset about many things, when only one thing is necessary. Mary has chosen the better part, and it will not be taken away from her."
>
> —Luke 10:38–42

I wish I could say I see myself in the upstanding women of the Bible: in Mary's firm yes (Luke 1:38); in Mary of Bethany's emotional rawness and her generous dispensing of oil (John 12); in Ruth's unshakable devotion to her family (Ruth 1:16–17).

I wish I saw myself in the good and popular saints: in Bernadette's pure and childlike faith; in Thérèse's humble smallness; in Mother Teresa's all-giving selflessness.

But no, as I page through the stories of the women who have gone before me, I resoundingly see myself in anxious Martha. Martha, who is rebuked by Jesus. Martha, who chooses the lesser path—the path of bustling and busyness, of preparation and planning—rather than prayer. I am, in so many ways, Martha.

This spring we were given a very late-notice PCS (permanent change of station). While we knew a move was imminent as my husband finished a master's degree, we weren't part of a normal move cycle, so it wasn't until thirty days prior that we were given a location and a date to pack our bags and get out. What's more, the move took us from the West Coast to the East Coast—a reverse to the move we had completed just eighteen months prior—with two toddlers.

My head buzzed. I felt bad leaving our landlord in a pinch with no renters. I was sad to pull our daughter from her first school experience before the year concluded. I was anxious about a new and unusual location where housing options were slim. I was uncertain about how we'd fit in with the squadron community. And I was nervous about a cross-country drive while snow was still falling on the mountains we'd have to drive through. But rather than reckoning with those feelings and discussing them with God, with my husband, with our family, I sprang into action, as I do.

I started packing giant Rubbermaid tubs full of clothes by size and season. I mapped three different driving routes based on weather. I purged the linen closet and the toy chest. I stopped the preschool payments, notified the gymnastics instructors of our last lessons, and freshened my résumé. I looked for new preschools, a new parish, new pediatricians and dentists and salons. As my husband made his way down the DOD-issued checklist, I churned through the extensive internal checklist that keeps our life and home operational, regardless of the coast or continent on which we temporarily find ourselves.

All was going smoothly. We found a rental home from afar. We made our last pilgrimages to our favorite restaurants and parks. We said our final farewells. The packers were speedy yet careful. We were on schedule.

But the evening after our things were boxed and built into a cardboard fiefdom that filled our home, we checked into an Airbnb in our neighborhood to await the movers the next morning. It was unseasonably cold for temperate northern California, and when we arrived, we found the owners of the rental house had fibbed about the place having central heating. I looked at our two toddlers, shivering in their little fleece jackets while they watched Disney+, and I broke down. My best-laid, long-agonized plans were falling apart.

I loaded the kids, their suitcases, the boxes of snacks and toys and electronics back into the car, drove back to our home, which was covered wall-to-wall and floor-to-ceiling with cardboard boxes, and threw blankets on the mattresses for our final night.

Once the kids had been shimmied in between the towers of boxes to their beds, my husband and I sat at the kitchen table, exhausted. But for the first time in weeks, I felt peace. There was nothing more to do. Nothing more to pack. Things had gone wrong—and yet, I felt we were where we were meant to be that night. Safe, cozy, and wrapped in the comforting embrace of a Father who provided, rather than chastised, even when I hadn't immediately turned to him.

Reflecting on this familiar story in Luke's gospel, I wonder if Martha's mistake isn't necessarily in her commitment to a to-do list. She shows hospitality and generosity by inviting Jesus into her home. She shows self-sacrifice and diligence by preparing a place for him. Where she errs, I suspect, is that she prioritizes those tasks *before* sitting with the Lord.

Same goes for me. Being organized and diligent isn't a sin, especially in military life where chaos seems to crouch around every corner. I hope that by buzzing behind the scenes, I am helping make life smoother and more predictable for our family, which I see as part of my calling as a mother and wife. The line gets blurred, however, when we believe ourselves to be self-reliant, rather than God-reliant. When I believe it is *my* work, *my* efforts, *my* will, that allows us to thrive. While it is good to lean into the skills and gifts we have to reduce our family's stress, we must remember those gifts are ordered toward service, not control. And we must not let our busyness overwhelm our prayer.

And that is where the arrow pierces my heart. Each move, I notice a marked change in my prayer life, in my marriage, and in my internal peace. I replace my time in Eucharistic Adoration with organization. Instead of ending my day in prayer or meditation, in the weeks leading up to a move, I almost always drift off to a restless sleep as I go through the litany of tasks that I have self-prescribed—many of which, my husband gently notes, are unnecessary.

He's right. I could have left the clothes for the packers. We took the first route I mapped. And selling our items on Facebook Marketplace garnered little profit for the time spent. The time, energy, and anxiety I spent on these tasks were well intentioned, but I could have spent that time with God. I could have chosen, as Jesus says, "what is better."

Back to my pal, Martha. Seeing my reflection in her has always troubled me, and I feel a twinge whenever I read that story from Luke. But after six weeks of hotel stays in fifteen states, we landed at our new home and our new parish where one Sunday we read another gospel about Martha—this time, in John's gospel (11:19–27):

> Many of the Jews had come to Martha and Mary to comfort them about their brother [Lazarus, who had died]. When Martha heard that Jesus was coming, she went to meet him; but Mary sat at home.
>
> Martha said to Jesus, "Lord, if you had been here, my brother would not have died. But even now I know that whatever you ask of God, God will give you."
>
> Jesus said to her, "Your brother will rise."
>
> Martha said to him, "I know he will rise, in the resurrection on the last day."
>
> Jesus told her, "I am the resurrection and the life; whoever believes in me, even if he dies, will live, and anyone who lives and believes in me will never die. Do you believe this?"
>
> She said to him, "Yes, Lord. I have come to believe that you are the Christ, the Son of God, the one who is coming into the world."

I wonder here if Martha's response of faith reflects a lesson she learned. After Jesus rebukes her for her busyness, she drops everything when she hears he's headed into town and runs to him. She's disappointed and frustrated that Jesus did not prevent her brother's death, but her belief is not shaken. She knows who Jesus is. She knows who she is. She knows what faith promises, even if she misinterprets how and when and what is about to happen.

That hope is there for me, and you, too. We are bound to fail and sin and misstep. We will not achieve perfection no matter how many to-do lists, shopping trips, or road maps we plan out. Even when we are distracted and bumbling and white-knuckled as we force our will and our plans, when those inevitably fail, Jesus welcomes us back into his arms, time and time again, and gives us what we really need.

Questions for Reflection

1. Think about the PCS seasons you have experienced. What has gone well? What has not?
2. Which of your God-given talents lends itself to the moving process? What about your spouse? How can you better lean on God in the midst of those challenging transitions?
3. How have you felt God's providing care in the midst of one of your moves? What sustainable practices could help you become more grounded in his presence during these times?
4. How can you keep your eyes and ears open for other families navigating a move? Who is new in your community, and what kind of support might they need? How might you respond, or connect them to others?
5. In what ways can you see yourself in both Martha and Mary from the gospel passage that opened this chapter? Or is there another Bible figure or saint who comes to mind as an example you admire?

Ξ Chapter 8

THE HARD PARTS + SHELTER

God is our refuge and strength,
    a very present help in trouble.
Therefore we will not fear, though the earth
    should change,
    though the mountains shake in the heart
      of the sea;
though its waters roar and foam,
    though the mountains tremble with its
      tumult.
There is a river whose streams make glad the
    city of God,
    the holy habitation of the Most High.
God is in the midst of the city; it shall not be
    moved;
God will help it when the morning dawns.
The nations are in an uproar, the kingdoms
    totter;
    he utters his voice, the earth melts.
The LORD of hosts is with us;
    the God of Jacob is our refuge.
Come, behold the works of the LORD;
    see what desolations he has brought on
      the earth.

He makes wars cease to the end of the earth;
    he breaks the bow, and shatters the spear;
    he burns the shields with fire.
"Be still, and know that I am God!
    I am exalted among the nations,
    I am exalted in the earth."
The LORD of hosts is with us;
    the God of Jacob is our refuge.

—Psalm 46:1–11

When I talk about the challenges or "hard parts" of our military life to civilian friends and family, the first questions are always about deployments: When did he deploy? For how long? Is he scheduled to go again? And yes, periods of extended absence bring hardship, loneliness, strain on families. But there's more to it, and it's worth naming the intangible ways this life can hurt.

Periods of absence can foster other challenges: intemperance, resentment, temptation, infidelity, gluttony. These run far too rampant in our communities, though we try to hide and silence them.

We rarely speak of the financial insecurity that can come with military life. We don't like to think about how the people who serve our country can go off to war and leave their families with food stamps and the hope that it will be enough. Few of us talk about or openly acknowledge how we can be sent to places where we can barely afford housing, where the base housing is unsafe or unsanitary, where the schools are ill-equipped, where we know no one.

Some people in our military community have seen terrible things—things of war and death and destruction. Others have comforted a loved one who has been forever altered by those encounters.

Many of us have experienced the loss of our loved ones and been forced to mourn alone because time and distance and finances meant we couldn't grieve with family or friends. So too are we likely to miss weddings and births and baptisms of the people we cherish. It's not uncommon to feel ostracized and detached from our people and the places we once called home.

There are assignments we do not want. We beg and plead to God, to commanders, to friends, *Please change it. Do not make me do this.*

There are people we cannot tolerate. Who bring us hurt and disrespect, and to whom we somehow owe obedience.

There are people with whom we build community, then assignments or distance or even arguments pull them out of our life, leaving a wound or hole.

Some of us mourn the what-ifs and the what-could-have-beens. We wish our children better knew their grandparents and aunts and uncles. We long for an extra set of hands, a trip to the grocery store unencumbered, a night out without a hundred-dollar babysitter bill. We grieve the life that we had once dreamed of.

In military communities, there are persistent issues with sexual assault. With unemployment. With greed and envy and pride.

Big, small, temporary, permanent—the challenges range the gamut. Even writing this list feels so unbearably heavy. So heavy that I considered glossing over them, but no, the reality of this life is that it is so very hard. That it comes with extra burdens, extra worries, and extra pain.

What's perhaps most isolating is that the parts that are hard are different for all of us. My husband's first deployment went down easy, but the early days of motherhood knocked the wind out of me. I remember looking at a neighbor and wondering how she juggled her brood of littles so effortlessly, only to learn she was carrying a heavy cross in another relationship. We all have hard parts, and it can surprise us when and where they pop up. Even things that seem small—a week or two of night shifts, a visit from family, unpacking the last boxes—can send us into a spiral.

In one of my hard parts, I fled to Adoration, looking for quiet and peace and comfort, though those things felt completely out of reach. If I'm being honest, I was looking for a place to cry alone.

In the darkness of night, I slid into a pew in the back of the church and flipped open my Bible as a prop to justify my presence and my weeping. The book opened to the words of Psalm 46, which opened this chapter. My tears gushed. It did feel like the mountains were falling into the sea. It did feel like the hills were shaking, like the life I knew was falling out from beneath me. And yet, the psalm starts by reminding us that "God is our shelter and strength."

There are times when that promise of accompaniment, of strength, of safety, feels empty. There are times you look heavenward and ask, "Where are you?" or "Why?" We identify with Jesus's cry from the Cross: "My God, my God, why have you forsaken me?" (Mark 15:34).

And I think that's where we find the solidarity of faith—that God's own son, in pain and torment and agony, felt abandoned, felt alone, felt so very wounded. He knows how to suffer with us because he chose to suffer for us. He knows how we feel in those moments of absolute pain. He does not judge us. He does not dismiss us. He does not tell us that even our little worries are not meaningful. No, he suffers with us. He cries with us. He mourns with us.

He is the friend who sits with us on the couch and holds us as we sob. He is the person who hands us a tissue to wipe our tears and snot. He is also the person who, once we are done, stands up and makes us a cup of tea or a snifter of bourbon. Like a good friend, he comforts us, and then he offers to serve us, to envelop us, to strengthen us so we can carry on.

Jesus revealed the depth of who God is to us. He is a healer. He is a protective father. He is a generous savior. He is a just king. He is a friend to those on the margins. These roles have all appealed to me in different seasons and scenarios. But in moments of true despair, I come back to the image of God as having wings under which I can take refuge.

Psalm 91 offers a prayer about God as our protector: "He who dwells in the shelter of the Most High, who abides in the shadow of the Almighty, will say to the Lord, 'My refuge and my fortress; my God, in whom I trust.' . . . He will cover you with his pinions, under his wings you will find refuge; his faithfulness is a shield and buckler" (Psalm 91:1–2, 4).

That psalm is often referred to as "a prayer of Moses, the man of God," which means people dating back to the time of Moses have shared our longing for God's protection. It is a universal experience in which we do not need to feel alone.

For me, the insistence in the psalm is comforting: "He *will* keep you safe. . . . He *will* cover you. . . . You *will* be safe." Not he could, or he can, or he might if you are really good and faithful. Instead, it is stated with certainty that he will, as long as we turn to him.

It's comforting to know there is a place I can hide, I can cry, I can recover. There is a place where, amid the malice and bewilderment and blundering humanity of this world, I can be safe. There is eternally, unshakably, unquestionably somewhere I am seen and loved and cherished, even when it does not feel that way on this side of heaven.

We all will eventually need to find this place. We will likely need it more than once. So be confident in knowing that it is there. Be confident in going there. God *is* there.

Questions for Reflection

1. How would you name the hard parts you've experienced in this life?
2. What have been your spouse's hard parts? How have they aligned or not?
3. How do you each cope with your hard parts? Discuss.
4. Are there any tips you would share with someone in one of those hard seasons now? What keeps you anchored in God's providing love?
5. Flip through the Book of Psalms. Do any others stick out to you? Read them aloud. What do they tell you about God? What do they tell you about the people who wrote these words, who search for God?
6. Do you believe you can turn to God in your hard times? Why or why not?

Ξ Chapter 9

PRE-DEPLOYMENT PREP + PATIENCE

> To every thing there is a season, and a time to every purpose under the heaven: A time to be born, and a time to die, a time to plant, and a time to pluck up that which is planted; A time to kill, and a time to heal; a time to break down, and a time to build up; A time to weep, and a time to laugh; a time to mourn, and a time to dance; A time to cast away stones, and a time to gather stones together; a time to embrace, and a time to refrain from embracing; A time to get, and a time to lose; a time to keep, and a time to cast away; A time to rend, and a time to sew; a time to keep silence, and a time to speak; A time to love, and a time to hate; a time of war, and a time of peace.
>
> —Ecclesiastes 3:1–8, KJV

This Advent I decided I wanted to recommit to the peace, quiet, and waiting of the season, rather than the flurry of shopping, activities, and travel that typically decorate our days. Still, I have two toddlers. I was hosting my extended family for the holiday. And I had a book to write. No matter, I thought; I'll just get ahead of things.

So the minute I trashed the kids' Halloween candy, I set to clandestine Christmas prep. I had to be secretive so my husband, who is very strict on his "no Christmas until after Thanksgiving" policy, would be none the wiser. I am not very sneaky, so this plan did not go unseen, but he let me be and only gave an occasional eye roll.

Before we lit the first purple candle, I had many of the stocking stuffers squirreled away in the recesses of our closet, had sketched out an itinerary for our out-of-town guests, had a rough menu set, and felt at peace with our Christmas plans.

But then I realized the kids probably needed one more gift. We needed new chairs to replace the stained and wobbly ones for our dining table before guests arrived. We had more guests than plates, so we needed a new set. I needed to address Christmas cards. We should see Santa. The list grew, albeit at a less frantic pace, but somehow my nights got less silent as I tackled the to-do list I swore I wouldn't have this season.

It reminded me of the time before Trent's first deployment. Months before they were scheduled to leave, I remember another spouse in the squadron asking the commander's wife for a packing list. *Hm,* I wondered, *should I already be purchasing and packing for him?* I asked around, and sure enough, many spouses had been prepping for months! They had bought sheets and blankets and towels, gadgets and gizmos, sound machines and stationery (though I wonder now how many of those airmen actually wrote home). What's more, friends told me they had already finished their wills and powers of attorney as well as exchanged passwords and plans for who would manage the finances and insurance and bill payments. They had prepped their children. Written "Open When" letters to stuff inside their spouse's suitcases. And a litany of other items I had not yet considered.

My head spun. The deployment was still months away! We still had several TDYs and weekend getaways and daily life to live until then. But not wanting to be negligent, I asked my husband if we needed to hustle and catch up.

Now, my husband is far more go-with-the-flow than I am, which admittedly is not a high bar to clear, but in this instance he was firm: No. We would not start prepping. He shared a valuable lesson he now uses when he's instructing flying students: Parkinson's Law. This is a decades-old observation by a naval historian that states that "work expands so as to fill the time available for its completion." Or, in short, you will use up whatever amount of time is allotted to you to do any given task. In his experience, if he gives students two hours or two days for preparation, the end product will be the same—even if they had extra time, they will have spun their wheels for far too long, noodling and nitpicking extraneous details. And so, he often cuts their preparation time to encourage them to master efficiency, time management, and the self-reflection needed to know when they've done enough.

Applied to my own life, I know that a four-week or four-month writing deadline often produces similar results, with just more or less hemming and hawing, and maybe a little procrastination on my part. And giving my kids five minutes or five hours or five days to clean their playroom will result in the exact same level of mess.

The same was true for deployment preparation. I could have spent six months prepping, keeping in the back of my mind that I should grab extra deodorant or toothpaste at the grocery store, or making little mementos to tuck in his suitcase, but the trade-off would have been that I worried about his deployment for months ahead of time. It would have idled in a portion of my brain and kept me chronically on edge, constantly mourning and emotionally bracing. Instead, a few weeks before, we created a list, tackled that list in a matter of days, and then it was done. We traded a few days full of meetings, errands, and yes, a little stress for months of peace and presence.

It's a theme and an issue recurrent in military life—there seems to always be a slight buzz or vibration in the back of our minds, a niggling that something needs attention. I'm always just slightly aware that a move is on the horizon, a new house is needed, a litany of TDYs will come, change is brewing. It may manifest as a chronic scroll of Zillow, a habitual mulling on where we might want to go next, or vigilant, if not obsessive, preparedness. This isn't to cast stones: given the nature of our life, it makes sense that we are a people always standing on our tippy toes, looking to the horizon for a glimpse of what's next.

But as we see in Ecclesiastes, there is a time and season for each given thing. We shouldn't weep in a time for laughter. We shouldn't look ahead during a time of presence. As I reflected on this, I thought about how we don't start Lent's fast early. It would be silly to mourn before the time is right. So too, we don't celebrate the Easter season in advance, just because we know it will come. In liturgical living, we hold fast to the season we're in at that given moment, and for good reason. That reason is so we can most fully live in it. The same is true in our lived, everyday existence. We ought to be right where we are. And if we have questions about the season we're in, the answer is simple: prayer.

Hope, as we'll read in the next chapter, is what most sustains us during a deployment, long absence, or challenging season. And to find and root ourselves in hope, we must first steep ourselves in prayer.

And it's funny—as I think of my husband's synopsis of Parkinson's Law, I realize I see my faith life as this long, extended deadline that I'm often content to procrastinate. I have convinced myself I have all the time in the world to pray and work on my relationship with God, and that the tangible, earthly to-do items are somehow more pressing. But if we live in the present, we quickly realize the season of prayer is, and always is, *now*. And there is nothing more important.

Time spent praying before a deployment is critical, perhaps even more critical than buying sheets and sound machines. Sure, that prayer can mean time at Mass and Adoration, learning to pray as a couple or family, Confession, and silence to ponder and listen. But prayerfulness can also lead to something more, beyond these tangible practices—it can establish a season of peace that allows you to spend time with family, lavishly loving them before time away. The season of preparation can mean date nights, finding ways to serve one another, and openly working through your fears and apprehensions together. It can mean investing in friendships that will offer mutual support during the difficult time away. It can mean prioritizing bucket-list items in the weeks and months before, from as small as one last visit to a favorite restaurant to something big like a getaway where you invest time in one another. That's to say, preparation can mean a deeply steeped presence, rather than an anxious anticipation of what is to come, and prayer can initiate this peace.

Just a few weeks before my husband left on his first months-long deployment, he was offered an opportunity to do a flyover at a Notre Dame football game. As an alumnus and die-hard fan, it had been a dream of his from the first moment he sat in a plane.

Had we been worried about packing and preparing, he may have turned it down. He may have felt there was too much to do, too little time. Instead, we both jetted off to South Bend, him in a fighter jet and me in a Southwest 737. It was among the best weekends of our life. He got to accomplish a lifelong fantasy, and I got to watch him do it, basking in jet fumes and the reverie of how our life had unfolded since we had graduated and left the campus. The joy and photos and memories sustained us through many of the hard months ahead.

The bottom line is this: in preparing for a life-changing event like a deployment, a move, or a change, it is important we don't get lost in the preparation. We must not fill our days with busyness and bustling just to feel like we're accomplishing something. All that activity could be coming from a desire to manage something that feels outside of our control. The only antidote to insecurity in these big transitions, however, is trust in God.

That trust can be cultivated by staying rooted in the here and now. By being present to our families and to God. By offering him our fears, our anxieties, and our anticipation, rather than trying to manhandle it ourselves. The root of the problem is that rather than turning to God, we turn to our own self-reliance. If we're honest, perhaps we trust our own efforts more than we trust God's care for us—perhaps our obsessive preparation is coming from a fear that we are on our own.

Now, that said, there are real arrangements to be made. A will, while emotionally trying, is an absolute must. The legal team on base can help with that as well as creating a power of attorney, which is essential for everything from, say, renewing your lost military ID while your partner is out of the country to accessing accounts in your partner's name. On top of logistical financial considerations, there is also spending to consider. Sure, a little extra money might come in during the deployment, so how do you both envision spending it?

There are likely things to buy: sheets, pillows, shower shoes, sound machines, etc. But keep in mind that living spaces are tight, and excess can be more troublesome than simplicity. The same goes for sending packages—knickknacks may be more frustrating than helpful.

And there are emotional plans to be made: How often can you talk or text or email? For how long? What about time zones? When you are each stressed, and how can the other best comfort you from afar? How can you both remain rooted in faith under stress? What or who might trigger negative emotions, and what is your strategy for responding? What might each of your social lives look like during a deployment? Is there anything the other might do that would make you uncomfortable? And what about your spiritual preparations? Have you both gone to Confession? Prayed together? Prayed for one another? Had honest conversations with God and with your partner about what the next few months might look like? Those conversations are hard to have, I know, but they're harder over spotty Wi-Fi or text. If we are going to dwell in any kind of preparation, this might be the place to land.

If this feels like a lot, it is. But the sixth chapter of the Gospel of Matthew offers a prayer for us, for God: "Our Father in heaven, hallowed be your name. Your kingdom come, your will be done, on earth as it is in heaven. Give us this day our daily bread, and forgive us our debts, as we also have forgiven our debtors. And lead us not into temptation, but deliver us from evil" (Matthew 6:9–13).

Let us trust in God's will, not ours. Let us trust that he will give us our daily bread. And let us ask him to forgive us, and to lead us away from the temptations of self-reliance, of worry, of mistrust. Let us believe that, with him at the center, with simplicity in prayer, in action, and in preparation, we will serve him and us better than we can imagine.

Questions for Reflection

1. How do you typically prepare for things? Are you slow and methodical, or prone to a last-minute flail? What about your spouse? What might work best for your family?
2. How has your preparation style changed over time? How might it continue to transform?
3. What questions or fears do you have in the preparation process?
4. What role do God and faith play in that process for you?
5. Think of the areas of life that require preparation: physical, mental, emotional, etc. Which one comes most naturally to you? What might be a challenge? What about your partner? Discuss.
6. Read through Jesus's other teachings in the sixth chapter of the Gospel of Matthew. What else resonates with you?

Ξ Chapter 10

DEPLOYMENT + HOPE

> We are afflicted in every way, but not crushed; perplexed, but not driven to despair; persecuted, but not forsaken; struck down, but not destroyed; always carrying in the body the death of Jesus, so that the life of Jesus may also be made visible in our bodies.
>
> —2 Corinthians 8–12

I remember the 3 a.m. alarm clock sounding in the darkness. We had both been awake for some time, staring at the ceiling in silence. But the alarm meant it was time.

While he showered and put on his flight suit, I bustled about the dark kitchen, a single bulb lighting my way. I remember wondering what one is meant to pack for someone as you say a long farewell. A Gatorade and a granola bar felt like a woefully inadequate gesture of love and care. So I threw in a peanut butter sandwich. And a water bottle. And a handful of other mismatched items from the pantry, hoping that if I shoved enough things into a grocery bag, that would somehow make me feel I had done all I could.

When he came into the kitchen, we held hands and said a quiet Hail Mary before getting in the car and driving off into the dark night.

There's nothing left to say in those moments, so we drove in silence, all the way to the squadron. I hugged him with all my might as tears streamed down my face. We exchanged "I love yous" and a final kiss, and then he was gone.

Until he wasn't. Not five minutes later, as I stood hugging a friend in the parking lot, he reemerged.

"I'm canceled. We'll try again tomorrow," he said matter-of-factly. I dried my eyes and we drove home.

We tried tomorrow. And the next tomorrow. And a handful more. By the fourth or fifth attempt, I mentioned it may be time to check in to the base hotel so we didn't have another emotional faux-parting. When he finally did take off, days after our first solemn goodbye, some of the wives lined the runway with signs that read "GTFO" or "Finally!" The humor was a welcome balm to end a painful week and kick off a long six months.

It turns out that first week taught some good lessons applicable to most deployments, namely, humility, flexibility, and above all, that the plan never holds (it didn't on the way home, either). But that doesn't mean the plan, and in particular, *his* plan, isn't good or isn't worth trusting.

I promised at the outset of this book that I wouldn't ask you to silver-line the hard things. And I won't. There are immense burdens for both the active-duty member and the family during an extended period away. There are lonely holidays. There are long weekends where the kids are sick and there are no reinforcements coming to help. Something will break—a car, the furnace, a roof, a limb. You might be juggling new tasks, or relinquishing control over ones you've always managed. There is guilt in leaving your family behind, and outright fear for them if the worst occurs. And there is a heavy mental and emotional toll that comes with either being somewhere dangerous or someone you love being somewhere dangerous.

But that is why I love Paul's letters from prison—Ephesians, Colossians, Philippians, and Philemon. Paul wrote these books while he was in prison, and perhaps that is why they are so often associated with hope, faith, love, joy, and patience. He was imprisoned multiple times in multiple locations before his eventual beheading, but all the while, despite his circumstances, Paul speaks with radiant hope.

Hope is our call as children of the resurrected King. We are meant to look upon the Cross—its pain, its agony, its fear, its betrayal—and we are meant to see it all as the path to hope, to a future of eternal life.

So too would I claim that that hope is our call as military families.

Yes, we endure separation from those we love. Yes, we worry and agonize. Yes, we grow frustrated from dropped FaceTime calls, scarce food in the mess hall, and shifting timelines. We feel unmoored and unstable as we try to keep our life as normal as possible. It all feels off. But to wallow in that, to mourn for what should be, for me at least, was not the right path. Instead, we can choose hope.

We can hope for safety.

We can hope for smooth departures and returns.

We can hope for protection from temptation.

We can hope for strength and patience and grace.

We can hope that the military mission and our Christian mission align somewhere in the chaos.

We can hope that whether we are on the war front or home front, we are following God's call.

And we can hope that in the end of the deployment, of our time in the military, of our lives, we will be moving toward the ultimate gift of life everlasting.

What's more, after the Resurrection God sent us the Holy Spirit to help us turn our hope into action. In the Gospel of John, we read about the gift of the Holy Spirit:

> On the evening of that first day of the week, when the doors were locked, where the disciples were, for fear of the Jews, Jesus came and stood in their midst and said to them, "Peace be with you." When he had said this, he showed them his hands and his side. The disciples rejoiced when they saw the Lord. Jesus said to them again, "Peace be with you. As the Father has sent me, so I send you." And when he had said this, he breathed on them and said to them, "Receive the Holy Spirit. Whose sins you forgive are forgiven them, and whose sins you retain are retained." (John 20:19–23)

This reading that tells the story of Pentecost is so relatable. The apostles have just watched Jesus be killed by the Jews. And though they have heard Mary Magdalene's testament that Jesus is resurrected, the miracle of all miracles, they still feel scared. And so, in love, Jesus returns once more, this time to give them the Holy Spirit, who will empower them to do his work.

Even in the Easter season of jubilation and joy, I find myself looking at the Cross with worry, with agitation, and with stress. It would seem the Resurrection would be reason enough to hope, and yet, in my humanity, I, too, need more. And so, I turn to the Holy Spirit.

What's amusing is my husband and I were married on Pentecost Sunday. At the time, that fact meant little more to me than that there would be red banners and red flowers and red lights illuminating the altar, which, the priest astutely noted, would clash with my all-neutral color scheme. Now, years later, I wonder if the Lord knew I would need repeat infusions of the Holy Spirit to be a good wife, mother, friend, writer, and daughter, and so having Pentecost as a notable milestone in my own life would lead to, at minimum, annual reflection on the role of the Holy Spirit. In my life, that role is something of a buoy when I feel like I'm drowning. I often whisper for it under my breath with a simple prayer, "Come, Holy Spirit." The simplicity makes the prayer fitting in moments of frustration, joy, exhaustion, inspiration, and more.

The Holy Spirit was also important to Paul, the writer of those hopeful books in the Bible. When we read of his conversion, after he hears Jesus and is blinded on the road near Damascus (Acts 9), Ananias comes to meet him. Ananias says to Paul: "The Lord has sent me—Jesus himself who appeared to you on the road as you were coming here. He sent me so that you might see again and be filled with the Holy Spirit" (Acts 9:17). Immediately Paul can see. Immediately Paul believes. Immediately Paul begins preaching in the synagogues. He begins writing. Infused with the Holy Spirit, he becomes one of the most powerful forces of Christianity.

And that can be our call, too. When it feels dark, when it feels like we cannot see the way forward, when we are scared or distressed or sad, we can call to the Holy Spirit. Like a child calls to a parent during a thunderstorm, we can call out in fear and say, "Come, Holy Spirit. Come be with me." And when we make that call, we can hope—not in a flimsy sense of the word, but a hope rooted in belief and trust—that God will come.

Hope, therefore, brings us into greater communion with God, and all the good that streams from him. And isn't that what we all need when we're separated from our loved ones? Isn't that peace, that calm, that love, that home what we're so craving when we're sitting on the couch alone, awash in our loneliness and grief? It's still there. God will provide it, if we hope in him.

And here's the thing: hope, as is oft quoted, is a beacon to others. When you can flood situations with hope, others gravitate toward that light. The same is true of fear, anxiety, gossip, and frustration—they are contagious. When we choose hope and share it with others, we are answering our missionary call. We are living in the light of hope, and showing others how to do it too. We don't need to be preachy or inauthentic or boundlessly optimistic, just calmly rooted in the goodness of God and the fruits of his plan.

I hoped and prayed and pleaded for a fruitful deployment. After I finally watched Trent fly away, I drove home alone to alternate between sleep and tears. That night a bunch of the squadron wives went to see the Zac Brown Band. We dried our tears, lined our eyes, and threw on our cowboy boots with hopes for a fun girls' night. For whatever reason, the setlist was almost all the slow, sad songs, and we laugh-cried through the whole concert. It bonded us and gave us a hopeful way forward: together.

For the next six months, those same women—and several more—dotted our calendars with events to look forward to. We dressed up for a fancy Christmas party, complete with a dramatic reading of a rewritten classic, *The Squadron Who Stole Christmas*. We curated a playlist of girl bands and girl power songs and then booked a pub trolley to sing and laugh together. We saw *The Phantom of the Opera*. We had a weekly trivia date—and had quite a win streak!

I went home for six weeks, the longest I had been there since before I left for college. I spent time with friends I only see a few times a year. I actually helped my parents with holiday preparations, rather than flying in at the last minute. I had a sleepover with my grandmother where we stayed up "organizing" her old photographs, but really just gossiped about life back in Ireland.

And even Trent and I blossomed. Our communication skills, which had been honed during years of long distance, improved further. We practiced daily patience as we waited and searched for pockets of internet reliable enough to FaceTime. We learned to better speak each other's love language—while I would have preferred to send gifts and tokens of home, I learned clutter made him claustrophobic in his spartan living conditions. We had to get creative in how we bonded from afar, but it resulted in a seamless transition when he finally did come home.

And that's worth a note: there must be hope—but a tempered hope—for reintegration. Your reunion may not be Hallmark-card worthy. Those homecoming videos of parents surprising their kids at school are tear-jerking, but sometimes reunion looks more like searching the crowd for your spouse in an overcrowded hangar. Or picking them up at a civilian airport. Or them showing up at your doorstep unannounced. That is okay. It can still be joyful, if not photogenic.

So too, those first minutes and days and weeks home may be filled with awkwardness, tension, and confusion as you try to reblend your lives together after a period apart. It may not necessarily be a second honeymoon, but instead a relearning, a patience-building, a necessarily grace-filled period. As Paul pleads in yet another prison epistle: "I, therefore, the prisoner in the Lord, beg you to lead a life worthy of the calling to which you have been called, with all humility and gentleness, with patience, bearing with one another in love, making every effort to maintain the unity of the Spirit in the bond of peace" (Ephesians 4:1–3).

And in our case, patience, gentleness, and humility were needed at the end of Trent's deployment, too. The homecoming was as messy as his departure. People returned in drips and drabs over the course of a week or so. Trent was the last one back in American airspace. I can't say I handled all those moments of disappointment, of jealousy, of frustration with grace and patience, but looking back, it was one last opportunity to practice trust, patience, and hope.

Questions for Reflection

1. Consider your experience and expectations for deployments. For what do you hope? What are the challenges and fruits of this time for you personally? How does a deployment impact your relationship with your spouse?
2. Where do you find hope? What stands in the way of hope?
3. Listen to the song "Lord of All Hopefulness." What sticks out to you? Why?
4. In his letter to the Romans, Paul writes, "I consider that what we suffer at this present time cannot be compared at all with the glory that is going to be revealed to us" (Romans 8:18, GNT). How might we apply his words to our lives during deployment?

Ξ Chapter 11

SERVICE + SERVANT HEART

> Not all of us can do great things. But we can do small things with great love.
>
> —St. Teresa of Calcutta

When I consider our little military family, and the roads that got us here, I realize how wildly different each path was.

At some point as a young teenager, Trent got in his head that life as an astronaut would intrigue him. The best route to the moon and beyond was through the Air Force. And so he took flight lessons, applied for an ROTC scholarship, applied for pilot training, earned a fighter jet assignment, and began an illustrious, service-oriented career in the Air Force.

At a similar phase, I surmised I wanted to be a writer after taking a high school journalism class. My parents are both in the medical field, so without concrete advice on how to chase that dream, they suggested I flood my résumé with volunteer hours to better my college application. So I did. I made popcorn at juvenile diabetes walks. I sang off-key Christmas carols in nursing homes. I taught religious education to a classroom of wild fourth graders preparing for their first Reconciliation. And I spearheaded a toiletries collection for a doctor in my dad's practice who was serving overseas as part of his Army Reserves commitment. Even with the exposure, the military never—and I mean not for a fraction of a second—crossed my mind as an option for me. But the service component stuck.

And maybe that's what made saying yes to Trent's marriage proposal—not just a yes to him, but a yes to a life of moving and uncertainty and change—tolerable, if not attractive. Without having to serve in the military, or as St. Teresa puts it, doing a "great thing," I would consistently find other ways to serve others.

Daily life for military families is service by small things. We serve by our surrender and our sacrifice and our humility as we look at a picture much larger than ourselves. Yes, that all comes into play in the big moments, in assignments and deployments, but there are small, day-to-day sacrifices as well. We rarely know when, or even if, my husband will show up for dinner. He likely won't coach one of our kids until his years in the military (and thus bands of night shifts, TDYs, and last-minute schedule changes) are done. We'll repeatedly struggle to build deep roots in communities where we may only stay for months or years. My career will inevitably have to work flexibly around his. These aren't monumental crosses, but they are undoubtedly small ones that wedge into our lived reality. And every military family can enumerate theirs.

There are more concrete ways to serve, too. For a long time, I made meals I could drop on doorsteps of new parents all around town. Then I was asked to apply my nonexistent math skills to work the base auction that supported educational scholarships for military dependents. Then to serve on the board of the then-Officer and Civilian Spouses' Club. Then to be a key spouse. And still, I did not even scratch the surface of all the ways you can volunteer in a military community. Many bases have a thrift shop, where proceeds go toward educational scholarships. The Tax Assistance Center is always looking for seasonal volunteers. There are bases that allegedly have opportunities in fire, forestry, and fish and wildlife management. Or, when the time arrives, roles as a Command Spouse come with training and volunteer hours. If you need extra incentive, many on-base volunteer opportunities provide childcare.

With opportunities aplenty, why is service so important? Because to serve is to love others, which is what Jesus asks us to do, what the saints model for us, and what the Church empowers us to do. And to love others, we must know others. As Mother Teresa said, "I want you to be concerned about your next-door neighbor. Do you know your next-door neighbor?" The best way to know them is to witness them in their struggles firsthand. Just as Jesus visited and ministered to those on the fringes, so must we.

As we drop off a meal, when we see a mother in her days-old pajamas and unwashed hair, laundry piled on the couch, baby screaming from a bouncer, we can glimpse the gift of self she is pouring into that infant, that life.

As we sign checks for educational scholarships or witness a family counting their food stamps in the commissary checkout line, we can pray for those dreaming and sacrificing for a better future.

When we sit next to the widow at Mass, we can pause and ask her how she is truly doing with a willingness to listen to a tale or two of loneliness.

We can visit a fellow new neighbor in the depths of depression, and offer to help unpack the moving boxes still lining the walls months after she moved in.

We can escort a soldier to the chaplain or the mental health clinic when we notice something is amiss. We make certain he has all the resources he might need.

We can bake cookies for deployed service members and include a note that they are seen and loved and prayed for.

Or we can look to our parishes, our communities beyond the base's walls, or the wider world. There are infinite ways to serve others. And this comes back to our identity and our call as Christians: The way we serve can be finely tuned to our talents, our skills, our beliefs.

There are plenty of spouses who bristle at being asked to volunteer. They may feel that the military has failed to budge from its 1950s-era traditional roles and relies on a milspouse volunteer force, which hinders a milspouse *work* force. And there is truth in that complaint. But our volunteering should not grate at us. It should fall in line with who we are.

We can consider the vast litany of saints:

The mystic Teresa of Ávila was not asked to brave the rugged wilderness of Molokai to care for the lepers in lieu of St. Damien—she had her own work to do in Ávila.

The traveling St. Francis Xavier was not called to stand still and hold open St. André Bessette's door.

St. Oscar Romero was not called to be quiet. St. Joseph was not called to be loud.

We are all called to serve. We are not all called to serve in the same way.

St. Thérèse of Lisieux summarizes it beautifully in *The Story of a Soul*: "I understood that every flower created by him is beautiful, that the brilliance of the rose and the whiteness of the lily do not lessen the perfume of the violet or the sweet simplicity of the daisy. I understand that if all the lowly flowers wished to be roses, nature would no longer be enameled with lovely hues. And so it is in the world of souls, Our Lord's living garden."

The saints were all called according to their time and talents. So are we.

Even set roles can take different forms. When I was a brand-new spouse, at one of my first social gatherings, it came up in conversation that I worked. Noses were turned. Comments were made, including, "Husbands who have wives who work should never be made commanders. Their partners don't have adequate time to volunteer."

It grated on me at the moment, and after many years of reflection, I still disagree with that sentiment. I have witnessed command spouses who treat the command spouse role as a full-time job. They love and plan and care for the spouses who fall under their purview. It is a wonderful gift to be looked after in that way. But so too have I been blessed by the example of working command spouses. Those women continued to bravely forge their own paths, even when it was hard. Their time may have been more limited, but their model was just as valuable. They showed me how Trent and I could each pursue our own dreams, and do it alongside one another.

In both examples, these women chose to make the role right for them. And that is the ultimate lesson: we can serve whole-heartedly, sustainably, and fully when we serve according to our callings.

I had a friend who lived an hour from base, worked full time, and could rarely make social events, but she still wanted to serve our squadron spouses. She volunteered to send every spouse a birthday card.

Another was a mom with two kids under the age of two. She had limited time, but did possess a math degree. She used it to streamline the bank account our squadron spouse group used to host events and make charitable donations.

Another sewed the rank patches on every single desert flight suit for an entire squadron when the local seamstress backed out.

Another hospitable friend rallied together Catholic moms to say the Rosary every other week at the church playground so the kids could play while their moms prayed.

These are little actions, already in line with each one's skills, which they volunteered to apply with great love. They are examples of a tailored, personalized response to the universal call to serve. It may not seem like much, but these little moments of assistance allow us to live better together, to flourish together as we each bring our talents to the communal table. And what a feast it is when we can partake of others' generosity and skill.

That feast brings us to greater humility, too. When we serve others, we put our egos away. We must be willing to let go of our needs and desires in order to accommodate those of another. If done right, it is a constant act of humbling ourselves.

From that humility springs the greatest love, but we must empty ourselves in order to be filled by it. We realize God is the source of our love, our service, and we give because it is the best way to fully participate in that love.

This brings us back to our family's path to the military: my children will never know another life. At least not for a while. But when they are old enough to look back, I want them to see how both of their parents served others, each in their own way, according to their own calling, both with abundant love.

Questions for Reflection

1. What opportunities for service naturally spring to mind as places where you could make an impact on other people's lives? Are any a good fit?
2. What are some of the roadblocks to serving, and serving with a full heart?
3. Think of the saints. Which ones capture your imagination? What is it about their mission and faithfulness that appeals to you? How might you emulate them in your own way?
4. Consider the corporal works of mercy: feed the hungry, give drink to the thirsty, shelter the homeless, clothe the naked, comfort the sick, visit the imprisoned, bury the dead. What are some ways that you might bring natural talents and interests to some of these needs as they appear in your community?
5. For further biblical reflection, consider Jesus's call to action to Simon Peter in John 21:15–16. In short, if we love Jesus, we are to feed his lambs and tend his sheep. What might it look like for you to answer that call in the circumstances of your life right now?

Ξ Chapter 12

THE FUTURE + RE-DISCERNMENT

Now the boy Samuel was ministering to the LORD under Eli. The word of the LORD was rare in those days; visions were not widespread. At that time Eli, whose eyesight had begun to grow dim so that he could not see, was lying down in his room; the lamp of God had not yet gone out, and Samuel was lying down in the temple of the LORD, where the ark of God was. Then the LORD called, "Samuel! Samuel!" and he said, "Here I am!" and ran to Eli, and said, "Here I am, for you called me." But he said, "I did not call; lie down again." So he went and lay down. The LORD called again, "Samuel!" Samuel got up and went to Eli, and said, "Here I am, for you called me." But he said, "I did not call, my son; lie down again." Now Samuel did not yet know the LORD, and the word of the LORD had not yet been revealed to him. The LORD called Samuel again, a third time. And he got up and went to Eli, and said, "Here I am, for you called me." Then Eli perceived that the LORD was calling the boy. Therefore Eli said to Samuel, "Go, lie down; and if he calls you, you shall say, 'Speak, LORD, for your servant is listening.'" So Samuel went and lay down in his place. Now the LORD came and stood there, calling as

> before, "Samuel! Samuel!" And Samuel said, "Speak, for your servant is listening."
>
> —1 Samuel 3:1–10

Until it lit on fire in the midst of a hectic PCS, we had a Dyson vacuum with a transparent, cylindrical tank. As you hoovered the rugs, you could watch the dust particles, stray hairs, stickers, and Teddy Grahams get sucked up into the tube and then spin around and around in a contained tornado.

I was thinking about this vacuum and its pertinence to military life as I sat drinking coffee in the quiet one morning. I could identify with those spinning bear cookies. In the prior six months, we had just completed a mad-dash through a cross-country, six-week PCS, followed by a series of weddings in Georgia, New Jersey, Michigan, and Ireland. Then we sprang into the holiday season—once again gassing up the car for a road trip to see family for Thanksgiving before scrambling home to frantically adorn the house to host Christmas. Add in some TDYs and a string of preschool viruses, and I can attest that frenetic is not strong enough a word for our tempo.

In some ways, that's been our life from the start of this military adventure. In our pre-marriage years, my husband and I dated long-distance while he went through pilot training and I got my writing career moving. Whenever we scraped together enough money or vacation days, one of us would hop on a plane to visit the other.

Once we were married, we were keen to explore our new home in North Carolina. We'd rustle up a group of friends and hit the beach, the mountains, wherever we could drive. We traveled to one of our families for every holiday, for weddings, for so many TDYs. Truly, a suitcase was, and often still is, almost always in a state of being half unpacked and half re-packed on the floor of our bedroom.

Even with young kids, we didn't let up. We capitalized on our eighteen-month California assignment and rented an RV to explore the Pacific Northwest. On long weekends we reunited with far-flung friends in Lake Tahoe, in Long Beach, in Monterrey, in Napa. I am enormously thankful for the adventures and experiences our vagabond existence has afforded us. Because of the impermanence of our living situations, we are quick to jump at opportunities to explore, to marvel, to experience. And I do wonder if military life speaks to people like us who are willing to wander, motivated by adventure, and who seek something *more*.

When I reflect with both exhaustion and gratitude on why we are in constant motion, I remember that our lifestyle also makes it hard to live near the people we love most, so instead we try to go to them when we can. We jump on a plane to celebrate milestones. We get on an interstate when someone is sick. We schedule trips to reunite with dear military friends from whom we've been separated. We try to find windows when we can replicate our childhood memories with our kids and their grandparents. I find myself trying to give them what I had, even while living a life so unlike what I grew up with.

Now in living that double life—as a military family and a civilian one—there are days it truly feels like we're being spun inside a vacuum. Days I lose track not just of the day, but of the month and year. But then I wonder what life will be like when we turn off the vacuum, when we cut ties to the military, buy a forever home instead of a series of rentals, build friendships with neighbors and classmates and establish roots that stay put for years, ascend professional ladders in one corporation, maybe even have family nearby. What will that life even look like? Will we still feel fulfilled? Will we still work toward something meaningful? Will we have regret? Will we itch for the antics military life afforded? Does that grass just look greener from here?

I think we all wrestle with these questions—whether we leave our military experiences at four years or fourteen or twenty-four. We are irrevocably divorcing ourselves not just from a job, but from a lifestyle, from a community, from a way of living and being. It's a scary plunge, and one that's hard to come back from.

Over the years we've weighed, shuffled, and reconsidered just how long we'll be here, doing this job, living this life. A trusted commander once wisely advised my husband and me to jump in with both feet, one way or the other, to commit to retirement or to get out as soon as possible so we could start anew. We ignored that sage advice. We've never come to a concrete decision of when his military service will end. We waffle and wonder. We make up our minds only to change them. The pros never outweigh the cons, nor the reverse. That's why this reading in Samuel is such a good fit for this chapter. As we've asked and pondered and prayed about our future, I've often been jealous of Samuel, who gets direct contact with God.

But as I reread this passage for the hundredth time, it finally hit me: when he receives his summons in the temple, Samuel is sleeping with the ark of the covenant. He is devotedly pursuing God—to the point of putting his body next to God's word—before God speaks to him. And maybe that commitment to put himself in proximity to God is where we differ. It made me question whether I truly, devoutly make time, space, and quiet for God. Or if I expect God to grab the dirty pot and sponge from my hand and say, "Excuse me, could I bother you for a moment to chat?" Do I assume that he will quiet the children's pleas and squabbles when he has something to say to me? And do I hope he will stop me from scrolling mindlessly on my phone so I am forced to look to him instead?

I think I do. If I am honest with my deepest self, I think I hope that the bridegroom wants me so deeply that he will interrupt me to demand my attention, rather than patiently waiting for me to turn to him. I want him to scream out rather than offer a quiet invitation. And I suppose he could do any of those things, but instead, he gives all of us the free will to choose to come to him. We have to take the first step.

And that's a scary position. It's like asking someone out on a date—we're putting our hearts on the line, praying we won't be scorned. And then we have to sit by the phone waiting for a response, wondering if we'll get any response at all. If we carry wounds of rejection, that first step can feel like a monumental leap. Waiting in the silence for God's voice can be so scary that we avoid it altogether, numbing or spinning ourselves in busyness to avoid the quiet.

God's silence is not an abnormal fear. St. Teresa of Calcutta talked of "the silence and the emptiness" on the other end of her prayer. The Carmelite St. Teresa of Ávila wrote about her multi-decade interior darkness, and has been quoted as saying, "If this be the way you treat your friends, no wonder you have so few of them." Even Jesus on the Cross seems to experience a moment when he doesn't feel the internal consolation we all seek, when he worries he has been abandoned.

I think we so desperately want communion with God, but before we commit to it, we want to know he wants us too.

So where do we seek him with the hope of hearing his voice speaking to us? Let's look at another prophet, Elijah:

> He said, "Go out and stand on the mountain before the LORD, for the LORD is about to pass by." Now there was a great wind, so strong that it was splitting mountains and breaking rocks in pieces before the LORD, but the LORD was not in the wind; and after the wind an earthquake, but the LORD was not in the earthquake; and after the earthquake a fire, but the LORD was not in the fire; and after the fire a sound of sheer silence. When Elijah heard it, he wrapped his face in his mantle and went out and stood at the entrance of the cave. Then there came a voice to him that said, "What are you doing here, Elijah?" (1 Kings 19:11–13)

I don't think it's an accident that God is not in the strong wind. He is not in the earthquake. He is not in the fire. He does not yell or plead or demand. He is in the silence, waiting to see if we persist. When I lay that notion on top of my own life, one of speed and flurry and movement, it's no wonder I don't often hear him. I'm not cultivating the time and persistence and silence to truly seek him.

Silence is frightening. In silence and in prayer we are confronted with the thoughts we'd rather not think, the events we'd rather not relive, the sins we try to forget, the weaknesses we pretend don't exist, and our fears and anxieties about the future. Maybe we even sense that the direction in which God is leading us isn't where we want to go. And so, we too often avoid that silence altogether.

In his discussion on mental prayer in *Time for God*, Fr. Jacques Philippe digs into our fear of silence and how it hinders our prayer. He writes:

> In fact, doing mental prayer necessarily means experiencing our poverty, being stripped of everything, feeling naked. In other kinds of prayer and spiritual activities there is always something to support us: a certain knowledge of how to do these things correctly, the sense of doing something useful, and so on. Even in community prayer, we can rely on the others. But in solitude and silence before God, we find ourselves unsupported, alone with the reality of our self and our poverty. Of course, it is very difficult for us to accept the fact that we are so poor; that is why people naturally tend to avoid silence.

I am so guilty of this. Though I try daily to quietly commune with God, it takes mere moments for my brain to zip to to-do lists and meal plans and who needs laundry done before school in the morning and that embarrassing scene from college more than a decade ago and how I could have responded better to that email this morning and so on and so forth. I can hear the little ping, ping, ping of the pinball sliding up, down, and sideways around the recesses of my mind, rather than quietly focusing on God. Even as I reset time and time again to quiet, it is a muscle that needs constant attention and exercise because I so rarely use it. My hope is that in time, it strengthens, and I can find silence and therein hear God speaking to me.

So too do I hope that silence becomes more natural in our life after the military as well. Even when the moving is done, and the paintings are hung on their last walls, and we don't change dentists every year, and the friendships are solidified, and, truly, if I stop creating endless to-do lists in the name of normalcy, I know I'll still have to cultivate silence as a discipline. And if I can create a habit of silence, perhaps it won't be so frightening. Maybe in it I'll even find comfort and presence.

Maybe in that silence, when we do cut the ties that bind us to the military, we'll once again have to reassess who we are. We'll have to find time for quiet so we can ask God who he intends for us to be *now,* after all we've seen, experienced, and learned. And in some ways, this re-discernment of our vocation brings us full circle. We're back to that first chapter, to our identity being defined by our relationship with God rather than our service or our families or jobs or anything else.

And at that core, one thing remains: we are beloved. We are desired. And whatever the next phase holds, that is one thing that will never change.

Questions for Reflection

1. Go back to the stories of the prophets Samuel and Elijah in this chapter. What sticks out to you about their encounters with God? How do their experiences call you to sharpen your perception of God's presence in your daily life?
2. What do you believe God is calling you to in this season of life? How can you stay in tune with what God wants for you?
3. Where or how do you best experience communion with God? What helps or gets in the way of those moments?
4. When you think about life after the military, what types of emotions arise? What types of dreams, fears, anxieties do you have?

5. When you look back at a life in a military family, what gifts have you been given?
6. If you were to write a prayer for military life—a prayer of thanksgiving, lamentation, praise, or intercession—what might yours sound like? What aspects of this life would you lift up to God, and how?

Ξ Conclusion

YOU ARE A WILLOW

> As you therefore have received Christ Jesus as Lord, continue to live your lives in him, rooted and built up in him and established in the faith, just as you were taught, abounding in thanksgiving.
>
> —Colossians 2:6–7

As I mentioned in the introduction, I wrote this book as I've been navigating this military life right alongside you. My journey as part of a military family is far from over. In my own life, some of the stages we've covered are happening now, and some are yet to come. Some we might even double back to.

And that's part of it—both the military life and the Christian life are not linear. We progress for a season, only to regress. We climb a hill, only to slide back down a bit. We chart a course, get lost, and end up back where we began. It's all a squiggly line that goes forward, backward, up, down, crosses over, and ends up in places you didn't know it could go. And so a conclusion feels wholly premature, when there is so much yet to do, see, learn, and grow from.

As we carry on in this life, I find comfort in the number of resources available—for both the military and Christian lives. I've mentioned many of my favorites in these pages, but there is an endless font of faithful writers, producers, podcasts, artists, apps, and more who bring great thoughtfulness and clarity into the world, each in their unique way. Go find the ones that speak to you. They will bring great inspiration, comfort, and companionship.

And the military has wonderful resources too. Back when I was a key spouse, I got training on all the base resources we had at our disposal. They ranged from couples counseling to lactation support to educational scholarships to vacation discounts to childcare resources. Frustrations aside, the military is not blind to the challenges of this life, and they are trying to fill gaps. But it is up to us to chase down the appropriate solutions.

These two lives, that of a Christian and that of a military family member, intersect in so many ways—or at least that's what I intended to outline here. My personal hope is that you'll continue to identify, experience, and abide in that overlap in your own life after reading along with me. While there is a temptation to live these two lives as separate layers, or on separate days, like hats we take on and off depending on the weather or situation, we are better off to clothe ourselves in all that we are. We are more whole when we are not segmenting ourselves. The truth is that our experience in military families can make us better Christians. And being a faithful Christian can make us a stronger military family. When we let these roles intersect and overlap, we become more authentic in all of them.

Our life is one of chronic dualities: trust and worry, hope and grief, strength and weakness, faith and doubt, heaven and earth. We can hold both. And God can, and will, hold us in both, as long as we are rooted in him.

And so, if we are not lifeboats just along for the ride, perhaps we're instead something with deep roots—roots that grow when we're living our best, most authentic versions of ourselves. Something that might sway, but not break. Something that may wither for a season, but then bursts into bloom anew. Something that provides respite, healing, peace, strength, hope. For me, the image that comes to mind is a willow.

The willow is mentioned repeatedly in the Bible. As we see in Leviticus, the early church uses willow branches to rejoice and grow closer to the Lord (23:4). In modern times, the Orthodox church uses willows, like at Palm Sunday, as a symbol of new life. But for a poetic meditation, I'll share one last passage from Ezekiel:

> Then he took a seed from the land,
> placed it in fertile soil;
> a plant by abundant waters,
> he set it like a willow twig.
>
> It sprouted and became a vine
> spreading out, but low;
> its branches turned toward him,
> its roots remained where it stood.
> So it became a vine;
> it brought forth branches,
> put forth foliage.
>
> There was another great eagle,
> with great wings and much plumage.
> And see! This vine stretched out
> its roots toward him;
> it shot out its branches toward him,
> so that he might water it.
> From the bed where it was planted
> it was transplanted

to good soil by abundant waters,
so that it might produce branches
and bear fruit
and become a noble vine. (Ezekiel 17:5–8)

Let us become the willow vine. The vine that turns toward him. The vine that sends roots deep into good soil. The vine that produces good fruit for him.

As you go forward, I'm praying for you. I'm journeying with you. And I'm giving thanks for you. Thank you for accompanying me, too.

BIBLIOGRAPHY

De Sales, Francis. *Introduction to the Devout Life.* TAN Books, 1994.

Philippe, Jacques. *Time for God.* Scepter, 2008.

Thérèse of Lisieux. *The Story of a Soul: The Autobiography of the Little Flower.* TAN Books, 2010.

Tara McMullen is a freelance writer, editor, and assistant producer of the University of Notre Dame's Emmy Award–winning "What Would You Fight For?" videos.

McMullen earned her bachelor of arts degree in English and French from the University of Notre Dame. After graduation, she served as an associate editor of *Notre Dame Magazine.* You can find her work in *Our State, Military Spouse* magazine, *Notre Dame Magazine,* Blessed Is She, *Life: Beautiful,* Mothering Spirit, and more.

She lives in Florida with her husband, who is stationed there as an Air Force fighter pilot, and their two children.

Founded in 1865, Ave Maria Press, a ministry of the Congregation of Holy Cross, is a Catholic publishing company that serves the spiritual and formative needs of the Church and its schools, institutions, and ministers; Christian individuals and families; and others seeking spiritual nourishment.

For a complete listing of titles from

Ave Maria Press

Sorin Books

Forest of Peace

Christian Classics

visit www.avemariapress.com